Disability

Key Concepts

Published

DISABILITY

Colin Barnes and
Geof Mercer

Polity

The right of Colin Barnes and Geof Mercer to be identified as author of this work has been asserted in accordance with the Copyright, Designs and Patents Act 1988.

First published in 2003 by Polity Press in association with Blackwell Publishers Ltd, a Blackwell Publishing Company.

Reprinted 2004

Editorial office:
Polity Press
65 Bridge Street
Cambridge CB2 1UR, UK

Marketing and production:
Blackwell Publishers Ltd
108 Cowley Road
Oxford OX4 1JF, UK

Published in the USA by
Blackwell Publishers Inc.
350 Main Street
Malden, MA 02148, USA

A catalogue record for this book is available from the British Library.

Library of Congress Cataloging-in-Publication Data
Barnes, Colin, 1946–
Disability / Colin Barnes and Geof Mercer.
        p.   cm. (Key concepts)
        Includes bibliographical references and index.
        ISBN 0-7456-2508-8 — ISBN 0-7456-2509-6 (pbk.)   1. Sociology of disability.   2. People with disabilities.   I. Mercer, G. (Geoffrey) II. Title. III. Key concepts (Polity Press)
        HV1568 .B34 2003
        362.4—dc21   2002007084

Typeset in 10½ on 12 pt Sabon
by SNP Best-set Typesetter Ltd., Hong Kong
Printed in Great Britain by MPG Books Ltd, Bodmin, Cornwall
This book is printed on acid-free paper.

Contents

1
Disability: A Choice of Models

For most of the twentieth century in 'Western' societies, disability has been equated with 'flawed' minds and bodies. It spans people who are 'crippled', 'confined' to wheelchairs, 'victims' of conditions such as cerebral palsy, or 'suffering' from deafness, blindness, 'mental illness' or 'mental handicap'. The individual's impairment or 'abnormality' necessitates dependence on family, friends and welfare services, with many segregated in specialized institutions. In short, disability amounts to a 'personal tragedy' and a social problem or 'burden' for the rest of society.

However, from the late 1960s, this orthodoxy in thinking and practice became the target of campaigns across Europe and North America. Disabled people, particularly those forced to live in residential institutions, took the lead in calling for policy changes. Their demands highlighted the importance of much greater support for 'independent living' in the community (Hunt 1966a; Brattgard 1974), and in the United States also assumed a civil rights focus (DeJong 1979). Disabled activists and organizations of disabled people were united in condemning their status as 'second-class citizens' (Eisenberg et al. 1982). They redirected attention to the impact of social and environmental barriers, such as inaccessible buildings and transport, discriminatory attitudes and negative cultural stereotypes, in 'disabling' people with impairments (UPIAS 1976; Bowe 1978).

By contrast, the academic literature broadly accepted the 'orthodox' view that disability is an individual and medical issue. Although gender and 'race' were by the 1980s generally recognized as distinctive causes of social oppression, this was not true of disability. Disabled critics dismissed prevailing accounts in the social sciences as irrelevant, 'theoretically backward' (Abberley 1987: 5) and resolutely 'disablist' (Oliver 1996b). 'There were no disjunctures between the dominant cultural narrative of disability and the academic narrative. They supported and defended each other' (Linton 1998: 1).

In this introductory chapter, we begin by outlining social science approaches through the 1960s and 1970s that analysed disability as a form of social deviance and sickness. Next, we trace the gathering critique by disabled activists and academics and the development of an alternative, sociopolitical approach to disability. Finally, we identify key issues in disability theory and practice for more detailed discussion in later chapters.

Disability as a personal tragedy

Twentieth-century social theory typically followed medical judgements in identifying disabled people as those individuals with physical, sensory and cognitive impairments as 'less-than-whole' (Dartington et al. 1981: 126), and hence unable to fulfil valued social roles and obligations. This incapacity left them 'dependent on the productive able-bodied' (Safilios-Rothschild 1970: 12). These and other negative associations meant that disability was perceived as a 'personal tragedy' (Oliver 1983). This encompasses an individual and largely medicalized approach: first, disability is regarded as a problem at the individual (body-mind) level; second, it is equated with individual functional limitations or other 'defects'; and third, medical knowledge and practice determines treatment options. From a societal perspective, disability is dysfunctional:

> the values which underpin society must be those which support the interests and activities of the majority, hence the

emphasis on vigorous independence and competitive achievement, particularly in the occupational sphere, with the unfortunate spin-off that it encourages a stigmatising and negative
view of the disabilities which handicap individuals in these
valued aspects of life (Topliss 1982: 112).

For most of the twentieth century, this personal tragedy
approach was applied in a variety of educational and charitable institutions and through medical and psychological
interventions. Indeed, large numbers of disabled people were
'put away' in segregated institutions on the grounds that it
was for their own good and to stop them being a burden on
others (Goffman 1961). Yet, in practice, institutional regimes
were often harsh, and long-term residents were liable to be
'written off' as 'socially dead' while awaiting the ends of their
lives (Miller and Gwynne 1972).

Disability and social deviance

The problematic aspects of disability from a societal viewpoint are vividly illustrated in functionalist analyses of health
and sickness. As outlined by Talcott Parsons (1951), sickness
is akin to social deviance, because it poses a threat to 'normal'
role performance and wider economic productivity and efficiency. This leads to the establishment of a sick role that
grants temporary and conditional legitimacy to the sick
person. It seeks to achieve a balance between acknowledging
'incapacity' and preventing 'motivated deviance' or malin-
gering. Society accepts that the sick person cannot get better
simply by an 'act of will' and he or she is permitted to with-
draw temporarily from 'normal' social roles. In return, the
individual must obtain medical confirmation of their condition and follow the recommended treatment, while agreeing
the importance of leaving the sick role behind as soon as
possible.

However, the applicability of the sick role to those with a
'chronic illness and disability' attracted widespread criticism,
because these conditions are defined as long-term if not irre-
versible. One response was to construct a separate 'disabled
role' (Safilios-Rothschild 1970) characterized by adjustment
to an extended but authorized dependency (Haber and Smith

1971). The individual is required to co-operate with rehabilitation professionals in order to achieve some degree of 'normality'. This describes a hierarchical relationship where the professional (helper) identifies the needs and capabilities of the lay (helped) person and prescribes appropriate individualized 'solutions' ranging from health and social care to special educational provision (Finkelstein 1983). Moreover, it adopts the profession's view of the 'ideal' patient as someone who defers to its knowledge and authority, and ignores the potential for contrary lay interests or expertise (Freidson 1970).

From a contrary theoretical perspective, symbolic interactionists stressed the social construction of what is perceived as deviance in everyday interaction:

> *social groups create deviance by making the rules whose infraction constitutes deviance*, and by applying those rules to particular people and labelling them as outsiders. From this point of view, deviance is *not* a quality of the act the person commits, but rather a consequence of the application by others of rules and sanctions to an 'offender'. The deviant is one to whom the label has successfully been applied; deviant behaviour is behaviour that people so label. (Becker 1963: 8; – emphasis original)

A significant benchmark for studies of social reactions to difference was Charles Lemert's (1951) distinction between *primary* and *secondary* deviance. Primary deviance arises where social norms or rules are broken but there are no long-lasting consequences. In contrast, secondary deviance generates a more significant and enduring social reaction that is sufficient to produce a deviant identity and status. Generally, the attribution of deviance to people with impairments is associated with 'ascribed' (involuntary) rather than 'achieved' (purposive) rule breaking. Nevertheless, particular groups, including black people and women, disproportionately attract specific psychiatric labels such as 'schizophrenia' and 'depression' respectively (Scheff 1966; Busfield 1986). Once applied, a medical label such as 'mental illness' at least confirms and at most transforms the public perception of an individual. It is also difficult to challenge or remove a medical label (Freidson 1965, 1970).

As a further illustration of the social construction of deviance, the 'recipients' of deviant labels must be taught how to act out their ascribed role. Professionals and specialized organizations are central to this socializing process. Robert Scott, in *The Making of Blind Men* (1969), illustrates how agencies responsible for the education and training of people labelled as blind reorganize the personal identity of their clients so as to conform to the professionals' image of a 'blind person', even though 'there is nothing inherent in the condition of blindness that requires a person to be docile, dependent, melancholy, or helpless; nor is there anything about it that should lead him to be independent or assertive' (Scott 1969: 14). New entrants are rewarded for conforming to staff expectations. They are praised for being 'insightful' when they do what the rehabilitation team wants, and are criticized for 'blocking' or 'resisting' when they disregard agency aims. This regime generally brings about a profound change from recruitment to completion of training. Nevertheless, as Scott demonstrates with case studies of Sweden, England and America, there are significant national differences in the roles and expectations of blind people.

The preoccupation among service providers with appropriate adjustment on the part of those with an impairment is again vividly illustrated in the application of psychological 'loss' or bereavement models. One of the most widely cited studies contains a four-stage process of psychological adjustment and rehabilitation to a severe spinal cord injury (Weller and Miller 1977). The initial reaction of 'shock' and horror is followed by 'denial' or despair that any recovery is possible, leading to 'anger' at others, and finally to 'depression' as a necessary preliminary to coming to terms with diminished circumstances. This 'acceptance' or 'adjustment' may not be reached until one or two years later. A parallel response trajectory has been identified for children with impairments attending a residential school (Minde 1972). Its key phases are 'disorientation' (following the loss of links with home and the local community), 'depression' (as the permanency of their impairment is confirmed by older pupils), 'anger' (at their difference from non-disabled peers), and finally, 'acceptance' (of the limitations of the disabled role).

The determinism of these 'adjustment to loss' models effectively sets aside the subjective experiences of disabled people and the specific socio-cultural and economic context (Albrecht 1976). While there is widespread agreement that there are often significant psychological (and other) costs associated with impairment, such models impose a 'psychological imagination' based on able-bodied assumptions of what it is like to live with an impairment (Oliver 1983).

Stigma: managing a spoiled identity

An associated feature of interactionist studies is their emphasis on individual coping or management strategies. Erving Goffman (1963) provides the classic study of responses to stigma, or a 'spoiled identity', including 'abominations of the body', with illustrations of those described as 'blind', 'deaf', 'crippled', 'deformed', 'disfigured', 'mentally ill' and 'stutterers'. He acknowledges that there is no necessary association between such attributes and their contemporary stereotype, but explores how the meaning of these marks of difference is negotiated through social interaction. In mid-twentieth-century America, he lists the benchmark 'identity norms' for a male as being 'a young, married, white, urban, northern heterosexual Protestant father of college education, fully employed, of good complexion, weight, and height, and a recent record in sports' (Goffman 1963: 128).

His characterization of 'abnormals' resonates with other social psychological writings on 'difference'. These highlight the 'liminality' of those on the margins of what society regards as 'normal':

> The long-term physically impaired are neither sick nor well, neither dead nor alive, neither out of society nor wholly in it. They are human beings but their bodies are warped or malfunctioning, leaving their full humanity in doubt. . . . They are neither fish nor fowl; they exist in partial isolation from society as undefined, ambiguous people. (Murphy 1987: 112)

Goffman's interest in 'undesired differentness' (1963: 5) centres on how individuals manage their 'spoiled identity' in everyday social interaction – what one sociological text refers to as the 'inevitable problems of living that confront the disabled as a result of their impairments' (Clinard and Meier 1989: 368). Encounters between 'normals' and 'stigmatized' people are characterized by immediate and often acute tensions for the visibly 'discredited', while for the 'discreditable' whose stigma is not immediately apparent the dilemma is whether or not to display their 'abnormality'. He documents a broad range of 'passing' (hiding the stigma) and 'covering' (reducing its significance) strategies to avoid embarrassment and social sanctions. These include repeated and often painful medical and surgical procedures to make the individual 'more normal' or less likely to attract a critical public gaze. The only other option for the stigmatized person is 'withdrawal' from social interaction.

Fred Davis, in a study of the social interaction between non-disabled people and those with a visible impairment, lists some of the points of tension: 'the guarded references, the common everyday words suddenly made taboo, the fixed stare elsewhere, the artificial levity, the compulsive loquaciousness, the awkward solemnity' (Davis 1961: 123). Nevertheless, he outlines a process of 'deviance disavowal' whereby the difficulties in social interaction are gradually 'normalized' over time. He identifies three main stages, starting with 'fictional acceptance', where interaction is kept to a minimum. A second 'breaking through' period begins when the stigmatized person encourages the 'normal' person to disregard their condition. The end-point is a 'normalized relationship' where difference is dissipated, leading to the seal of approval from a non-disabled person – 'I don't think of you as disabled' – so unthinkingly confirming the latter's tragic fate. The 'well-adjusted' disabled person is someone who lives up to non-disabled peoples' expectations as brave, cheerful and grateful when being helped. Conversely, they are quickly criticized if they act 'out of character' by being assertive and demanding.

The stigma label is further characterized by its potential to 'spread'. At the individual level, physical impairment is sometimes taken as an indication of a generalized incapacity – as typified by the 'Does he or she take sugar?' syndrome. In addition, negative attitudes and behaviour may be extended to other family members as a 'courtesy stigma' (Goffman 1963).

A general feature of this interactionist literature is its concentration on the defensive manoeuvrings of disabled people. This suggests that 'those stigmatised are apparently firmly wedded to the same identity norms as normals, the very norms that disqualify them' (Gussow and Tracey 1968: 317). However, there are exceptions: the treatment of disabled people is not always represented as benevolent, and not all disabled people take over the values of non-disabled people. In his study of life in a psychiatric institution, Goffman (1961) acknowledges that asylum inmates are 'colonized' and their supposed 'helpers' also act as jailers. He also outlines a continuum of potential responses to incarceration: from 'true believers' to 'resistors'. None the less, these examples are submerged beneath a general emphasis on achieving social acceptance and accommodating to the demands of 'normals'.

Deviance and social control

From a conflict perspective, studies of the social construction of disability took their cue from C. Wright Mills (1963), who argued that the definition of social problems must be located within wider material and political contexts, including the power relations and conflicts between dominant and subordinate classes. Historically, there was a trend away from judgements of social deviance rooted in religious criteria of 'badness' towards medical judgements of 'sickness'. The medicalization of disability confirmed the arrival of an orthodox medical profession, with State-legitimated authority in the delivery of health and illness services (Conrad and Schneider 1980). Over time, there has been a proliferation of other 'moral entrepreneurs' (Becker 1963), in education, psychology, counselling and social work, all seeking an enhanced role in services for people with accredited impairments.

The growing impact of professionals in general and medicine in particular on the lives of disabled people proceeded unevenly. It is most evident in studies of mental illness that include a full-blown critique of a self-serving profession (psychiatry) for exploiting its power of labelling and collaborating in a wider process of social control. From an 'anti-psychiatry' perspective, the concept of mental illness is dismissed as a 'myth', or at least a socio-political construct, but there was little discussion of alternative support paths (Szasz 1971; Ingleby 1981). By comparison, the medicalization of physical and sensory impairments attracted little if any criticism, but rather confirmed the existence of a 'caring society'.

Challenging the disabling society

It was largely left to disabled people to develop their own critique of the conventional approaches to disability. A key contribution in Britain was Paul Hunt's edited collection entitled *Stigma: The Experience of Disability* (1966b). This challenged the standard preoccupation with the medical and personal 'suffering' experienced by individuals with an impairment. In his own essay, Hunt argued that 'the problem of disability lies not only in the impairment of function and its effects on us individually, but also, more importantly, in the area of our relationship with "normal" people' (Hunt 1966a: 146) A sharp dividing line is drawn between the social lives and interests of 'able-bodied' and disabled people. The latter are 'set apart from the ordinary' because they pose a direct 'challenge' to commonly held societal values: 'as unfortunate, useless, different, oppressed and sick' (p. 146).

Disabled people are viewed as 'unfortunate' because they are unable to enjoy the social and material benefits of contemporary society. These include the opportunity for marriage, parenthood and everyday social interaction. The few exceptions are lauded for their 'exceptional courage', but this simply confirms the 'tragic' plight of the vast majority. Indeed, it is overwhelmingly non-disabled people who like to celebrate such 'triumph over tragedy' heroics (Dartington et al. 1981).

The perception of disabled people as 'useless' flows from their lack of engagement in mainstream economic activities. As a consequence of their failure to conform to 'normality', whether in appearance or in control over their minds and bodies, they are set apart as 'different'. Moreover, 'People's shocked reactions to the "obvious deviant" stimulate their own deepest fears and difficulties, their failure to accept themselves as they really are and the other person simply as "other"' (Hunt 1966a: 152).

The level and form of prejudice against disabled people amounts to being 'oppressed'. It is illustrated by the discrimination widely practised in the built environment, employment, leisure and personal relationships. Finally, disabled people clash with 'able-bodied' values in so far as they are defined as 'sick, suffering, diseased, in pain' (Hunt 1966a: 155). This represents everything that the 'normal world' most fears – 'tragedy, loss, dark, and the unknown' (p. 155). 'Being seen as the object of medical treatment evokes the image of many ascribed traits, such as weakness, helplessness, dependency, regressiveness, abnormality of appearance and depreciation of every mode of physical and mental functioning' (Zola 1993: 168).

What also now emerges is a contrast between the individual model's 'property' approach that equates disability with an individual's impairment and a 'relational' perspective that highlights how people with impairments are subjected to wide-ranging processes of social exclusion. Furthermore, the conventional absorption in 'personal troubles' gave way to a collective sense of injustice: 'We are challenging society to take account of us, to listen to what we have to say, to acknowledge us as an integral part of society itself. We do not want ourselves, or anyone else, treated as second class citizens, and put away out of sight and mind' (Hunt 1966a: 158).

Frank Bowe, in *Handicapping America* (1978), pursues a similar theme when he lists six major barriers to the social inclusion of disabled people. These are architectural, attitudinal, educational, occupational, legal and personal (or everyday problems ranging from few material resources to the stigma of having an impairment). Common experiences of exclusion led to disabled people's growing sense of themselves as an oppressed minority. Thus, the first national survey of disabled people in the United States in 1986 reported significant support for the proposition that disabled people are 'a minority group in the same sense as are blacks and Hispanics' (Harris 1986: 114). Disabled people were increasingly seeking to 'take control of the definitional and interpretative processes so that they can forge their own identities and manage their own lives' (Albrecht 1992: 78).

Building a socio-political model of disability

The criticism of 'able-bodied' society was first codified into a radical, alternative to the individual model by the Union of the Physically Impaired Against Segregation (UPIAS) in Britain. Its manifesto, entitled *Fundamental Principles of Disability* (1976), contains the fundamental assertion that society disables people with impairments, thus directing attention to the impact of social and environmental barriers: 'In our view it is society which disables physically impaired people. Disability is something imposed on top of our impairments by the way we are unnecessarily isolated and excluded from full participation in society. Disabled people are therefore an oppressed group in society' (UPIAS 1976: 14).

UPIAS's analysis of the disabling society is built on a clear distinction between impairment and disability (see box 1.1). A medical definition of physical impairment is adopted (and subsequently extended to include sensory and cognitive forms), in contrast to a definition of disability in socio-political terms, as 'the outcome of an oppressive relationship between people with . . . impairments and the rest of society' (Finkelstein 1980: 47).

Box 1.1   UPIAS definitions of impairment and disability

- **Impairment**: Lacking part or all of a limb, or having a defective limb, organ or mechanism of the body.
- **Disability**: The disadvantage or restriction of activity caused by a contemporary social organization which takes no or little account of people who have physical impairments and thus excludes them from participation in the mainstream of social activities (UPIAS 1976: 3–4).

This distinction enables the construction of a 'social model' or a 'social barriers model' of disability (Finkelstein

1993b). The line of causation is redirected. In the individual model, 'disability' is attributed to individual pathology, whereas this social model interprets it as the outcome of social barriers and power relations, rather than an inescapable biological destiny. Thus,

> an inability to walk is an impairment, whereas an inability to enter a building because the entrance is up a flight of steps is a disability. An inability to speak is an impairment but an inability to communicate because appropriate technical aids are not made available is a disability. An inability to move one's body is an impairment but an inability to get out of bed because appropriate physical help is not available is a disability. (Morris 1993b: p. x)

Moreover, instead of an individualistic regime of rehabilitation and personal care services, the 'disabling barriers' diagnosis suggests wide-ranging social changes coupled with alternative forms of service support and provision (Finkelstein 1993b). As Jenny Morris later argued: 'Our anger is not about having "a chip on your shoulder", our grief is not a "failure to come to terms with disability". Our dissatisfaction with our lives is not a personality defect but a sane response to the oppression we experience' (1991: 9).

The impact of socio-political analyses of disability can be dramatic:

> I think I went through an almost evangelical conversion as I realised that my disability was not, in fact, the epilepsy, but the toxic drugs with their denied side-effects; the medical regime with its blaming of the victim; the judgement through distance and silence of bus-stop crowds, bar-room crowds and dinner-table friends; the fear; and, not least, the employment problems. (Hevey 1992: 2)

None the less, the social barriers *model* is only a stepping stone to building a 'social *theory* of disability' (Oliver 1996b: 41). This demands in-depth answers to such questions as: 'What is the nature of disability? What causes it? How is it experienced?' (Oliver 1996b: 29–30). As disability is socially produced, it follows that it displays contrasting forms, both historically and between societies. At the same time, theoretical analysis of the structures and processes that bring about the social exclusion and oppression of people with impairments also identifies the necessary targets for a new disability politics geared to overturning the 'disabling' society (Finkelstein 1980; Oliver 1983; Abberley 1987).

Nevertheless, the scope of this new approach to disability must not be exaggerated:

> The social model is not about showing that every dysfunction in our bodies can be compensated for by a gadget, or good design, so that everybody can work an 8-hour day and play badminton in the evenings. It's a way of demonstrating that everyone – even someone who has no movement, no sensory function and who is going to die tomorrow – has the right to a certain standard of living and to be treated with respect. (Vasey 1992: 44)

Policy definitions and measures

In response to criticism that its approach to disability ignored social factors, including the disadvantages experienced by disabled people, the World Health Organization (WHO) produced its *International Classification of Impairments, Disabilities and Handicaps* (ICIDH) (WHO 1980). It offered the definitions shown in box. 1.2.

Box 1.2 WHO definitions of impairment, disability and handicap

- **Impairment**: Any loss or abnormality of psychological, physiological or anatomical structure or function . . .
- **Disability**: Any restriction or lack (resulting from an impairment) of ability to perform an activity in the manner or within the range considered normal for a human being . . .
- **Handicap**: A disadvantage for a given individual, resulting from an impairment or disability, that limits or prevents the fulfilment of a role (depending on age, sex, social and cultural factors) for that individual. (WHO 1980: 29)

In what disabled critics dismiss as a characteristically individual approach, 'impairment' refers to those parts or systems of the body-mind that do not function 'normally', while 'disability' covers those activities that the individual cannot perform as a result of the impairment. For example, blindness is a visual 'impairment' that causes 'disability' or difficulties in reading. The stress is on functional limitations in the performance of basic daily living tasks. These span locomotion, reaching and stretching, dexterity, seeing, hearing, personal care, continence, communication, behaviour and cognitive functioning.

Most of the novelty of the WHO schema lies in the interpretation of 'handicap'. This highlights the social consequences associated with an impairment and/or disability. It raises the difficulties in performing social roles, while acknowledging that these vary across social groups and cultural contexts.

The ICIDH definitions found immediate favour with many social scientists, but provoked considerable criticism from disabled people's organizations. First, the approach relies primarily on medical definitions and uses a bio-physiological definition of 'normality'. It disregards the impact of social criteria in informing judgements about whether body weight and shape, mental distress or cognitive functioning is 'normal' rather than 'pathological'. Moreover, the definition of 'handicap' ignores the social and cultural relativity in role allocation. For example, women might be rated as having a 'disability' but not be 'handicapped' because the society in which they live denies them the opportunity to engage in certain activities because these are not considered appropriate for females (Wendell 1996: 17).

Second, 'impairment' is identified as the cause of both 'disability' and 'handicap'. This privileges medical and allied rehabilitative and educational interventions in the treatment of social and economic disadvantages. It justifies the domination of disabled people's lives by health professionals. In contrast, disabled people increasingly argue that disability (as defined in a social perspective) is not a health issue, and therefore that health professionals are not the appropriate judges of their support needs.

This leads to a third criticism, that the ICIDH represents the environment as 'neutral', and ignores the extent to which disabling social, economic and cultural barriers are significant in the social exclusion of people with impairments. Even though social and environmental influences are recognized, these have little significance or credibility in the application of the ICIDH in service planning or provision. The overwhelming clinical focus dictates strategies for individual adjustment and coping. 'Unrealistic' hopes and ambitions are constrained. Whether a person is born with an impairment or acquires it later in life, the ICIDH reinforces socialization into a dependent role and identity, for lack of any other choice. Certainly, medical and allied interventions have had many positive outcomes for disabled people, but the ICIDH concentrates on diagnosing and treating the individual's 'limitation' rather than that person's social exclusion.

Widespread disenchantment among disabled people and their organizations, as well as criticism from mainstream medical researchers persuaded WHO to revise its classificatory scheme. This resulted in the *International Classification of Functioning and Disability* (WHO 1999), or, more 'popularly', ICIDH-2. It sought to incorporate the 'medical' and 'social' models into a new 'biopsychosocial' approach. The overall result is a 'multi-purpose' classification system that retains the concept of impairment in body function and structure, but replaces 'disability' with activities, and 'handicap' with participation. In addition, ICIDH-2 assumes that functioning, activity and participation are influenced by a myriad of environmental factors, both material and social. This opens up new possibilities for a socio-medical analysis of disablement, although it retains individualistic medical notions of disability and its causes (Hurst 2000).

Notwithstanding these developments, there is ample evidence internationally of the continued acceptance of the individual model of disability in policy circles. Thus, the 'functional limitations' approach is widely incorporated within anti-discrimination legislation (as in the USA and Britain), and it continues to inform surveys of the prevalence of 'disability' within the European Union (Barnes et al. 1999; European Commission 2001).

Issues and themes

C. Wright Mills (1970) argued that the sociological imagination has a particular contribution to make in helping us see how some seemingly 'personal troubles' are more appropriately understood as 'public issues' that link to the institutions of society as a whole (p. 14). The basic aim is 'to see the *social* in the *individual*, the *general* in the *particular*' (Bauman 1990: 10). The realization that apparently 'natural' features of society are both sustained and revised by human action allows for the possibility of 'alternative futures' (Giddens 1982: 26).

It is our task to demonstrate the merits and potential of social analyses of disability. This entails addressing issues that arise at individual, social (group) and societal levels (Turner 1987; Layder 1997). Furthermore, as the disability studies literature has grown over the last two decades, the initial dominance of interactionist and minority group perspectives in the USA, and neo-Marxist analyses in the British literature, has been contested. A wide range of disciplinary perspectives and theoretical interpretations, including feminism, post-structuralism and post-modernism, now competes for attention in disability studies.

Most specifically in the chapters that follow, we review key issues and themes in analysing disability. In chapter 2, we equate a 'social model' approach within the analysis of disability as a changing form of social oppression and exclusion. It gives a specific stimulus to historical perspectives on impairment and disability, most notably with the growth of industrial capitalism. This highlights the establishment of professional (especially medical) dominance and the resort to institutional 'solutions'. These trends are exemplified by the emerging discourse around 'normalcy' and difference, including the scientific identification of 'defective' minds and bodies. Chapter 3 outlines more of the contemporary empirical detail required to substantiate claims about disabled people's social oppression. The discussion spans key areas across the 'public' and 'private' domains, including education, paid employment, the built environment, leisure and 'right to life' issues. It also explores how far other social divisions such as gender and 'race' mediate disability as well as any life cycle patterns.

Recent calls to 'bring impairment in' to disability studies are addressed in chapter 4. These have generated intense debate about 'impairment effects', while overlapping with a considerable literature by medical sociologists on the experience and meaning of 'chronic illness and disability'. It merges with a burgeoning interest in difference and identity, and post-structuralist-inspired studies of changing discourses on the body. Cultural representation and the media are examined in chapter 5. This offers a counterweight to the structuralist focus in early social model debates by exploring the negative media images of disabled people that dominate (Western) cultures. We also examine attempts by disabled people to generate a more positive disability identity and culture(s).

Chapter 6 explores the exclusion of disabled people from mainstream political processes and institutions, and the policy responses adopted in liberal democracies, including equal opportunities and anti-discrimination legislation. It also illustrates the emergence of a new 'disability politics'. This raises important questions about how far impairment and/or disability can be the basis for a shared identity or political project, or the basis for a 'new social movement'. Finally, in chapter 7, we bring an important comparative and international dimension to the debates on disability.

Terminology

A critique of established definitions and language has been an understandable obsession for disabled people, given that disabled people's lives are so affected by 'official' definitions and meanings. In our view, widely used English words such as 'cripple', 'spastic' and 'idiot' have lost any semblance of 'technical' meaning and simply become terms of abuse or ridicule. Equally, common metaphors such as 'turn a blind eye' or 'deaf ear' to the world reinforce an impression of incapacity and abnormality. An alternative vocabulary has proved to be a source of endless debate, but here the phrase 'disabled people', rather than 'people with disabilities', is used because it signals our emphasis on the ways in which social barriers affect life chances. Nevertheless, we concede that key terms, including 'disability' and 'disabled people', often defy easy translation into other languages. Moreover, different historical and cultural experiences often thwart agreement among those who speak a common language, as a cursory glance at the American and British literature confirms.

Review

Academic discussion of impairment and disability in the social sciences has been slow to undercut the prevailing 'personal tragedy' orthodoxy. Socio-political analyses of disability owe their momentum instead to the pioneering studies of disabled activists and the growing politicization of disabled people around the world. A new, vibrant disability studies literature is now building alternative perspectives to the established, individualistic approach to disability. This includes criticism of conventional policy responses to disability as well as mainstream service provision. It has also highlighted the contrasting form and character of disability across specific social, cultural, economic and political contexts. At the same time, the emergence of analyses of disability as a form of social oppression has triggered new demands for political action.

2
Disabling Societies: Domination and Oppression

The emergence of socio-political approaches to disability reflects disabled people's claims that they experience significant and entrenched social oppression. Our discussion starts from the premiss that oppression is a structural concept, and that it is evidenced by a highly unequal distribution of material resources and uneven power relations and opportunities to participate in everyday life, compared to those available to non-disabled people. We also assume that the form of dominance, and how it is maintained, may range from the overt force exercised by some ruling groups to the embedded assumptions and practices of everyday life that may also produce deep injustices – hence our interest in incorporating notions of 'ideological domination' and discursive power. As social oppression is interpreted in several ways, or contains distinct aspects, we begin this chapter by outlining the usage adopted here.

We conceptualize disability as a form of social oppression akin to sexism and racism, although it exhibits a distinctive form, with its own dynamics – hence our aim in the second part of the chapter to explore the social creation of disability as a historically and culturally specific form of social oppression. We review accounts of the emergence of a 'personal tragedy' approach to disability in Western societies, and its association with the growth of industrial capitalism. In the final part of the chapter we consider broad trends in the social oppression of disabled people since the middle of the twentieth century.

Disability as a form of social oppression

In highlighting social oppression, disability writers have emulated anti-racist and feminist analyses by moving away from class-based accounts to explore historically specific relations of dominance between non-class groups (Brittan and Maynard 1984). Disability demonstrates its own distinctive set of dynamics, although these may on occasion interact with the processes of class oppression. Like sexism and racism, disablism expresses itself in exclusionary and oppressive practices at a wide range of levels: interpersonal, institutional, cultural and societal.

The identification of disablism as a specific form of social oppression stems from the subordination of people because of their impairment. People categorized in this way are marked apart as a distinct social group on the grounds of their perceived bodily deficiency or abnormality and treated differently: 'For disabled people the body is the site of oppression, both in form, and in what is done with it' (Abberley 1987: 14).

Historically, the oppression of other social categories, notably women and black people, has been justified in terms of their biological shortcomings and weaknesses. However, in the last quarter of the twentieth century these claims have been in general retreat. In stark contrast, there has been no such reversal in popular thinking or public policy with regard to people with impairments. There is a continuing and exclusive emphasis on the deficiencies of the disabled mind/body. Indeed, medical interventions such as surgery or 'mind-changing' medication remain acceptable ways of addressing disability – since the 'cause' is located in those with an impairment, rather than in the society or groups which discriminate against such individuals (Finkelstein 1993a).

The way in which contemporary analyses highlight oppression is indicative of a shift in the ways of theorizing political power and dominance. More traditional notions dwelt on the uneven distribution of material resources and life chances. However, oppression is not just about being on the receiving end of a tyrannical power. It is also effected through apparently liberal and 'humane' practices, including medicine, education, bureaucracy, leisure and consumer goods (Foucault 1977). Thus, people in their everyday lives act and think in ways that are 'oppressive' to disabled people, but do not always recognize their actions as having this effect.

Iris Marion Young (1990) differentiates five main aspects of oppression: exploitation, marginalization, powerlessness, cultural imperialism and violence. *Marginalization* refers to the systematic removal of a social group from the mainstream of everyday life, and includes material disadvantages, exclusion from the division of labour, institutional segregation, and denial of citizenship rights. Countervailing social policies provide some recognition of disabled people's marginalization, but these 'solutions' may themselves facilitate economic and social dependency through enforced reliance on welfare benefits and services. This overlaps with *powerlessness* as the realization of oppression, which confirms that people have little control over or choice in what to do with their lives. It is verified by a sharp divide between those who exercise authority or power (as in the case of professionals) and those who simply 'take orders' and lack authority or status.

These two aspects of social oppression are contrasted with the Marxist concept of *exploitation*, which is reserved for the social relations between dominant and subordinate classes in the sphere of production, whereby the exploiting group extracts material gains from other workers. Of course, it is hardly possible to profit from the exploitation of another group's labour if, like disabled people, it is only marginally involved in the paid labour market. Alternatively, it is possible to emulate feminist arguments that men appropriate women's unpaid (domestic) labour as in sexual reproduction and child rearing and thus exploit them.

Cultural imperialism is a further aspect to social oppression. In recent centuries, a marked divide between 'able-bodied' and 'disabled' people has been established at the cultural level. 'Able-bodied normalcy' is embedded in everyday thinking and behaviour as a privileged or desirable state of being. The notion of 'able-bodied' assumes normative or universal standards by which all other 'bodies' are judged. The disabled population is set apart, as 'Other', or as deviant in specific ways. 'In its identification of some groups with despised or ugly bodies, rationalistic culture contributes to the oppressions of cultural imperialism and violence' (Young 1990: 11).

The defining feature of *violence* and harassment in the oppression of disabled people is that it is systematic and widespread. Irrespective of whether it takes the form of physical or sexual attacks, eugenic policies or verbal ridicule, it is directed at specific individuals because they belong to a particular social category – the 'disabled'. Moreover, even the threat of violence is a source of considerable fear and restrictions on life activities of the group targeted.

In the discussion that follows, we assess the specific pattern and intensity of these several dimensions of the oppression of disabled people, and consider claims that disabled people experience a specific form of social oppression and exclusion that rests on the following foundations:

> At an empirical level, it is to argue that on significant dimensions disabled people can be regarded as a group whose members are in an inferior position to other members of society because they are disabled people. It is also to argue that these disadvantages are dialectically related to an ideology or group of ideologies that justify and perpetuate this situation. Beyond this it is to make the claim that such disadvantages and their supporting ideologies are neither natural nor inevitable. Finally it involves the identification of some beneficiary of this state of affairs. (Abberley 1987: 7)

Historical patterns and perspectives

Until recently, there have been few historical studies of disability, and existing contributions have been criticized as lacking theoretical sophistication or extensive empirical grounding (Bredberg 1999). Most stress the continuity of negative attitudes and practices towards those with perceived impairments, although some identify signs of more liberal and humanitarian attitudes and policies towards disabled people, at least in modern times. The latter concentrate primarily on improvements brought about by philanthropy, scientific medicine, social welfare and educational policies (Winzer 1993).

Histories of disability often start their journey in ancient Greece with its idealization of body shape and fitness linked to acceptance of infanticide for those born with visible impairments. The dread of impairment is reinforced by examples drawn from the Bible suggesting that it is a punishment for past sins. The negative picture gathers further corroboration in the denunciation of newly born children with impairments as 'changelings', or inhuman beings substituted by the Devil, by a continuous line of medieval clerics from St Augustine to Martin Luther. There is also ample evidence that everyday life and popular culture were permeated with views that associated impairment with evil and wrongdoing and as a source of ridicule, fear and pity (Ryan with Thomas 1980; Thomas 1982; C. Barnes 1997). A more nuanced picture is occasionally available, as in Henri-Jacques Stiker's (1999) grand historical journey, which provides enough evidence to convince that oppression is not a universal or consistent experience for people with impairments. While the force of 'cultural imperialism' is abundantly evident, a major shortcoming is that there are very few attempts to explore a material basis to this changing historical detail.

Industrial capitalism and disability

In one of the first attempts to advance such a theoretical framework, Vic Finkelstein, in *Attitudes and Disabled People* (1980), outlines a historical materialist account. This relates qualitative changes in social responses to impairment to three main economic-technological 'phases': pre-industrial (feudal society), industrial capitalism, and post-industrial society.

In the pre-industrial phase, activity is agrarian, or cottage-based. While most people with impairments occupy the lower ranks of the social hierarchy, they are expected to participate in economic life. Other writers on disability, such as Brendan Gleeson, agree that, 'whilst impairment was probably a prosaic feature of feudal England, disablement was not'

(1997: 194). Feudal social relations focused more on subsistence than wealth generation and accumulation, so that 'disabled people were regarded as individually unfortunate and not segregated from the rest of society' (Oliver 1990: 27). At the same time, 'peasant households could not afford to consider any bodies as unproductive' (Gleeson 1999: 83). It was accepted that differences in individual economic performance might force people to change work to accommodate their impairment, rely on begging and charity alms, or in the case of older disabled people unable to work, they might provide shelter to others in return for personal support (Pelling 1998).

Little evidence has been provided to substantiate claims that people with impairments were readily integrated into social life in feudal societies. Certainly, sickness and impairment were constant features of everyday life, although the high mortality rate among people with impairments greatly reduced the numbers otherwise reliant on community support. As always, impairments varied in how far they led to marginalization. Certainly, there are studies, particularly that of the island of Martha's Vineyard in Massachusetts, that illustrate how this small-scale, isolated, rural community in the nineteenth century acted in inclusive ways to the relatively high proportion of people with hereditary deafness. Most notably, substantial numbers of the local hearing population learned sign language (Groce 1985).

Finkelstein's second phase relates to the establishment of industrial capitalism in nineteenth-century Europe and North America. His suggestion of a qualitative shift in responses to impairment is replicated in what Mike Oliver (1990) terms the 'social creation' of disability as a personal tragedy with the rise and entrenchment of capitalism. Both writers highlight the spread of a free market economy, wage labour, and the change to mechanized systems of production. 'The speed of factory work, the enforced discipline, the time-keeping and production norms – all these were a highly unfavourable change from the slower, more self-determined and flexible methods of work into which many handicapped people had been integrated' (Ryan with Thomas 1980: 101).

This build-up of constraints on the employment of people with impairments led to the increased displacement of 'unproductive' disabled workers from the work-place, although this process was uneven and drawn out, rather than sudden. The person with an impairment was at a disadvantage because of the decline of traditional, local community and family-based support systems and values, and the rising importance of geographical mobility to find employment. By contrast, the rapidly expanding industrial towns and cities appear far less accommodating to disabled people. A case study of nineteenth-century Melbourne in Australia demonstrates a growing 'socio-spatial marginalization' of disability (Gleeson 1999). This encompassed the segregation of disabled workers into a diminishing number of specialized activities such as home working, handicraft production and street trading.

Disability as a personal tragedy

Finkelstein's primary aim was to explain the development of an ideology of disability that stressed 'personal tragedy, passivity and dependence' (Finkelstein 1980: 1). This was extended by Mike Oliver in *The Politics of Disablement* (1990), where he draws on the neo-Marxist literature to highlight the crucial role of a reinforcing ideology or 'mode of thought' – that is, a set of values and beliefs underpinning social practice, in sustaining social oppression: 'the disabled individual is an ideological construction related to the core ideology of individualism and the peripheral ideologies related to medicalisation and normality' (Oliver 1990: 58).

A key inspiration within these debates in the 1970s and 1980s was Antonio Gramsci (1971, 1985), with his analyses of the way in which dominant interests do not simply rely on force or coercion. Instead, they seek to win the 'willing consent' of the subordinate population and achieve a 'hegemony' in the ideological domain through their involvement in cultural production and consumption. Their success is evident when one way of looking at the world is accepted at a common-sense level as 'natural'. Gramsci also presumed a more complex relationship between material and cultural factors. Whereas other Marxists had described a single, all-enveloping dominant ideology, he allowed for the 'relative autonomy' of 'hegemonic' culture from dominant economic interests, and recognized the existence of 'subaltern' cultures and their potential for generating political resistance and change.

With the rise of industrial capitalism, the hegemony of 'able-bodied' normality became the yardstick for judging people with impairments as 'less than human' (Oliver 1990: 89). This view pervaded education, religion and the law. Most particularly, the negative representation of disabled people in Victorian literature, by eminent novelists such as Charles Dickens, impressed itself on the popular imagination. It is replicated in the twentieth century by film and television images of disability (Hahn 1989). A further crucial aspect of cultural imperialism is the importance of charity in the lives of disabled people across Europe and North America. It provides an enduring cultural message that helps perpetuate an image of helplessness and dependency.

A further crucial issue in European and North American countries has been the increased profile of the (local and central) state in addressing disability issues, particularly since the seventeenth century. Mildred Blaxter (1976) reviews this interplay between economic and humanitarian factors in the development of social policies. Deborah Stone further elaborates this argument in *The Disabled State* (1985), suggesting that industrializing societies (such as the USA, Britain and Germany) faced a dilemma over how to distribute goods, services and other rewards. Although the main criterion is employment status, not everyone is able or willing to work, hence a second system emerges geared to resource distribution on the basis of perceived needs. The dilemma for those administering policy has been how to determine who is a deserving case and properly part of the needs-based system.

The state has played a key role in establishing administrative categories that expressed a 'culturally legitimate rationale for nonparticipation in the labor system' (Stone 1985: 22). The English Poor Law of 1601 offered an early example, with its distinction between the deserving and undeserving poor, with disabled people generally categorized as 'deserving' cases. Over the next two centuries, the disabled element was refined to include the 'sick, insane, "defectives" and "aged and infirm"' (Stone 1985: 40). The last two centuries have witnessed a further 'widening and loosening' of the definition of disability (Blaxter 1976). Nineteenth-century target groups were supplemented by those with war-time injuries, while eligibility gradually extended to some industrial injuries, and then more widely to cover individuals with a range of 'chronic illnesses and disabilities'. The growing numbers entitled to disability benefits raised cost concerns, but there was also a clash in occupational perspectives, with 'unavoidable incompatibilities between medical definition systems, which ideally are individual, qualified and provisional and administrative categories which are necessarily rigid, dichotomous and designed for large groups of people' (Blaxter 1976: 10).

The involvement of the medical profession in disability has been central to the legitimation of a personal tragedy approach. Medicalization (or the application of medical knowledge to an increasing range of social problems) emerged as a key aspect in the social control of disabled people. It supplanted more religious and traditional approaches. While people in early modern societies consulted a range of lay and 'medical' practitioners about their health and general well-being (Pelling 1998), by the nineteenth century an orthodox medical profession had overturned this pluralism in healing practice. Its ascendancy was not only justified in terms of theories of disease and healing grounded in scientific knowledge claims, but reinforced by its location in specialized sites (hospitals and asylums). These established a further distance and hierarchy between professional experts and lay patients, with control over the recruitment, education and training of new practitioners. Equally crucial, the medical monopoly of health care was legitimated by the state (Jewson 1976; Larson 1977).

More generally, the late eighteenth and nineteenth centuries witnessed a wide-ranging institutional system of social control that extended beyond hospitals and asylums to include prisons, workhouses, industrial schools and colonies (Cohen and Scull 1983). Specific impairment groups who became identified as social problems, notably those designated as having a mental illness, became significant targets for incarceration. Andrew Scull (1979, 1984) provides a detailed picture of this symbiotic relationship between state policy and the achievement of a medical monopoly over mental illness allied to 'manufactories of madness'. He contends that the medicalization of 'madness' and its institutional regime proved 'functional' to the capitalist state in terms of both economic efficiency and social order. While industrialism and urbanism led to physical and 'mental' harm among the mass of the population, the rise of institutions, particularly where it was allied to medicine, offered reassurance that something positive and humane was being done for the 'deserving poor'. Nevertheless, the scale of confinement demonstrated considerable international variation: less evident in Britain than in its European neighbours such as France.

As far as disabled people were concerned, another key aspect to their institutionalization emerged with the development of segregated schooling for disabled children. The origins of 'special education' lie in the late eighteenth and early nineteenth centuries, initially for deaf children and then for those with visual impairments, followed by those labelled as 'feebleminded'. There were successive waves of expansion into the early decades of the twentieth century, leading to 'special schools' for 'crippled' and 'physically defective' children and for those categorized as 'educationally backward' (S. Tomlinson 1982; Humphries and Gordon 1992; Winzer 1993). The training provided confirmed public expectations of disabled adults as capable of only minimal social and economic participation.

The medicalization of disability and the growing emphasis on the education and training of disabled children and adults also signalled a crucial professionalization of disability that continued apace through the twentieth century. To many writers on disability, professionals have proved to be 'disabling' and self-serving, always looking to extend their influence to new areas and groups (Illich et al. 1977). Certainly, disability was not long in becoming an occupational territory reserved for professional 'experts' who laid claim to specialized, esoteric knowledge (Freidson 1970). Moreover, with the growth in disability services, an increasingly complex division of labour was established. This encompassed a marked expansion in the professions allied to medicine, such as occupational therapists and physiotherapists, as well as in the educational and social welfare fields. The end result for disabled children and adults was a widening professional involvement in their lives, over educational provision, entry to paid employment, eligibility for welfare payments, and provision of technical aids and equipment. While following a broadly materialist perspective in tracing the emergence of a personal tragedy approach to disability, it is important not to overstate the case. It is important to reject 'explanations' that resort to the 'logic of capitalism' or undercut detailed examination of the actions of key interests such as medicine by claims that they operate 'inevitably' as the 'agents' of capitalism (Giddens 1981). This denies any autonomy to the struggles between competing groups and interests, including what were on occasion clashes between different capitalist interests. The outcome of these struggles is neither pre-determined nor so easily categorized.

Discourses and bio-politics

Another perspective on medicalization and the growth of institutions was advanced by Michel Foucault. His writings have exerted a growing influence in disability studies, and offer a counter to accounts that interpret disablism as a direct reflection of capitalist/ruling class interests (Finkelstein 1980; Abberley 1987; Oliver 1990).

By contrast, Foucault (1980) highlights power/knowledge struggles, with the body placed centre stage. He concentrates on the way in which knowledge and meaning are produced through discourse or ways of organizing claims and assumptions. The operation of power/knowledge is explored in relation to specific institutional settings and 'technologies' or techniques, in ways that historicize discourse, knowledge and 'truth' (Foucault 1982). Scientific (rather than juridical or religious) categories, as produced in medical discourse, become the focus of analysis. He identifies a new technology of the body or disciplinary power. This new 'bio-politics' encompasses a shift from sovereign to disciplinary power (Armstrong 1983). Whereas the body had previously been physically or externally controlled, the emphasis now moved to mechanisms of self-discipline. The aim was a docile body that 'may be subjected, used, transformed, and improved' (Foucault 1977: 136).

This discursive approach displaced the individual as an independent, authentic source of meaning and action (Hall 1997). Moreover, the new medical 'scientific' discourse on 'normality' served both a clinical and a moral function: 'it claimed to ensure the physical vigour and the moral cleanliness of the social body; it promised to eliminate defective individuals, degenerate and bastardised populations. In the name of biological and historical urgency, it justified the racisms of the state ... It grounded them in "truth"' (Foucault 1979: 54).

Lennard Davis illustrates the Foucauldian project in *Enforcing Normalcy* (1995) when he argues that 'the social processes of disabling arrived with industrialisation' as a new set of discourses and practices (p. 24). These centred on the distance between 'normalcy' and the 'disabled body', with a particular influence exerted by statistics on medical knowledge and practice. What had been the dominant discourses around notions of the 'grotesque' and the ideal body in the Middle Ages were completely overturned by the normalizing gaze of modern science. This established a hierarchical standard for pronouncing some bodies and minds as abnormal and inferior – in terms of appearance and performance. Standards of physical health, mental balance and moral soundness became closely linked, so that defective bodies and minds were also associated with 'degeneracy' (Young 1990).

In the case of mental illness, the professional take-over has long attracted condemnation from social scientists, on the grounds that the growth of psychiatry has been self-serving. Thus, its dominance of mental health was 'neither warranted nor desirable', and ignored the social origins, if not also the social construction, of mental illness (Ingleby 1983: 143). In terms of psychiatric discourses, by the mid-nineteenth century, 'mental illness' was accepted as a generic term covering very different conditions. Entering the twentieth century, psychiatry extended its gaze from the psychoses to the neuroses (Armstrong 1983). It also moved outside the asylum into families, schools and work-places. A growing army of mental health workers in psychology, counselling, social work and education gained legitimacy, and the basis for social regulation shifted from 'dangerousness' to 'risk'

(Castel 1983; Miller and Rose 1988). This legitimated professional interventions around prevention and rehabilitation.

Davis (1995) provides a further detailed illustration of the transformation in discourse in a historical review of deaf people's emergence from their isolation in an overwhelmingly aural society and culture. He suggests that eighteenth-century Europe witnessed the 'invention' of deafness, in the sense that a novel philosophical-scientific discourse was established. The hearing world perceived the 'deaf and dumb' as particularly tragic, because of their inability to communicate and to think rationally. This was also a period when literacy and reading emerged as marks of distinction. The pursuit of enlightenment was a spur to establishing residential schools for deaf children. However, these became a discursive battleground between the advocates of sign language ('manualism') and those promoting lip-reading and speech ('oralism'), with 'Deaf people' stressing the importance of linguistic and cultural identification and solidarity, and critics underscoring assimilation rather than linguistic difference (Lane 1989; Baynton 1992). (For the purposes of this discussion, the use of the capital "D" denotes membership and recognition of a distinctive Deaf culture.)

Overall, professional discourses around impairment/disability targeted unruly or defective bodies as evidence of a lack of humanity. There was an emphasis on regulating the body, through socializing (controlling and self-disciplining), rationalizing (with a clear separation between natural impulses and rational behaviour) and individualizing (as a self-contained entity) (Shilling 1993).

Eugenics

With the spread of Darwinian ideas about evolution and 'the survival of the fittest', impairment became identified as a threat to social progress.

> We civilised men, on the other hand, do our utmost to check
> the process of elimination; we build asylums for the imbecile,
> the maimed, and the sick; we institute poor-laws; and our
> medical men exert their utmost to save the life of everyone
> to the last moment ... Thus the weak members of society

propagate their kind. No one who has attended to the breed-
ing of domestic animals will doubt that this must be highly
injurious to the race of man. (Darwin 1922: 136)

Several of the early, eminent statisticians – Galton, Pearson
and Fisher – promoted the eugenic applications of statistics
for 'improving the human race'. Initially, the merger between
statistics and biology promised a science of the average effects
of the laws of heredity (Abrams 1968: 89), but this interpretation of 'normality' gave way to the idea of ranking, with
those deviating from the norm located on a continuum from
higher to lower scores.

This is vividly illustrated in the case of Intelligence
Quotient (IQ) scores. They quickly acquired a moral connot-
ation of superior and inferior 'intellectual' functioning. Early
scientific interest concentrated on distinguishing between
'mental deficiency' and 'normality', but the application of
a normal distribution curve and new tests, such as the
Binet–Simon, led to the identification of 'mildly retarded' and
'moron' categories. Statistical theories reinforced a deter-
ministic account of intelligence, 'race' and human evolution.
Social Darwinists classified disabled people with 'severe'
impairments as 'mutants' (Radford 1994). The spectre of
'race degeneration' was fostered by John Langdon Down's
1866 classification of the 'mongolian idiot' as a throwback
to a non-Caucasian type (Gould 1980). Defective bodies and
minds were perceived as 'dangerous' and 'threatening' to the
rest of society.

Eugenicists further highlighted links between intellectual
and physical deficiency and a range of social evils, including
crime, vagrancy, alcoholism, prostitution and unemployment (Kevles 1985). Across Europe and North America,
policies espousing 'social hygiene' gained ground, ranging
from segregation in institutions to State and medically
sponsored schemes for sterilization and abortion. In 1938,
thirty-three American states had a law allowing the forced
sterilization of women with intellectual impairments, but in
Nazi Germany during the 1930s and 1940s an altogether
more systematic and extensive extermination programme was
introduced against the 'unworthy'. This led to the murder
of more than 270,000 disabled people on the grounds that

they were 'travesties of human form and spirit' (Burleigh 1994: 194).

Late twentieth-century trends

'Phase Three' in Finkelstein's (1980) account corresponds to mainstream accounts of the emergence of a post-industrial society in the second half of the twentieth century, with the new, computerized, information technology identified as the harbinger of significant social and economic changes. He interprets this as bringing altogether more positive opportunities for the inclusion of people with impairments in paid employment, so allowing 'the most severely physically impaired people . . . to live relatively independently in the community' (1980: 11).

In the 1990s, fresh momentum was given to claims about significant changes in late twentieth-century capitalism. Manuel Castells (1996) is one of those who argues that there has been a notable shift away from manufacturing and service industries towards 'informationalization' and an increasing global economy. However, most writers on disability are less sure than Finkelstein about the impact of these trends on the social inclusion of disabled people (Albrecht 1992; Roulstone 1998; Sapey 2000). Some believe that the replacement of the spoken by the written word, through changing forms of communication technology, and speech translation software will facilitate the inclusion of those with sensory and some physical impairments (cost considerations notwithstanding). Conversely, people with learning difficulties, mental health system survivors, and older disabled people may be further marginalized and excluded. Finkelstein's optimism notwithstanding, the consequences of the new informational economy seem far from clear, offering both an enabling and a disabling potential, and likely to divide disabled people in new ways.

From a non-Marxist perspective, Gary Albrecht (1992) also draws links between economic and technological changes and historical shifts in disability. He categorizes societies according to their technological subsistence base into hunting and gathering, pastoral, horticultural, agrarian and industrial (with post-industrial and post-modern stages). Each societal type is characterized by a distinctive set of relations between its biological, physical and cultural environments. This includes a unique 'type, incidence, and prevalence of impairment and disability and of social responses to them' (p. 39).

Albrecht's illustration of the American experience of industrialism provides a valuable corrective to accounts that focus exclusively on Western Europe. While there are significant similarities, the parts played by key interests, including the State, the medical profession, and private corporate interests demonstrate important differences, at least in emphasis (Berkowitz 1987). He acknowledges the significance of the medicalization of impairment and disability, but stresses how in a private insurance-dominated health care system people with impairments have become a huge market for the services and products of health and social care agencies and professions. These include aids and equipment, drugs and insurance, training and rehabilitation. 'The disability business focuses on both treating persons with disabilities as raw materials and by commodifying disabilities and rehabilitation goods and services, making them objects of commerce' (Albrecht 1992: 68).

The profit potential of the disability business has led to considerable competition between different factions of capital or groups within the dominant class. Marta Russell illustrates how, in what she terms the 'Money Model of disability' (1998: 96), the recent expansion of rehabilitation medicine and services, including the massive growth in residential (nursing) homes for disabled people, has turned 'entrepreneurial medicine' into a multi-million-dollar business. Throughout this period, the American state has played a facilitating role for private and professional interests without prioritizing public sector or publicly funded services to the same extent as in many European countries.

Notwithstanding these differences, disability policy has become an increasingly significant item for political debate. It was in the second half of the twentieth century that separate disability policies and growing numbers of disabled people dependent on services and benefits became established features of social welfare systems. However, disability policies became a primary target when governments across Europe and North America began to advocate a retrenchment in state expenditure in the late 1970s. These constraints re-kindled administrative battles over where to draw the bound-ary lines around eligibility and support needs. Capitalist states were caught between balancing financial interests and constraints with the maintenance of their political legitimacy and social order.

> Disablement makes an important contribution to the ideo-logical crisis surrounding health and welfare in capitalist societies. This is because disabled people, being both deserv-ing and expensive, pose a crisis of legitimacy for the State in those capitalist societies which seek to be both profitable and civilised at the same time. (G. Williams 1991: 517)

While restricting eligibility for, and cutting expenditure on, disability benefits and services provides a strategy for reduced spending, it is constrained by expectations among disabled people of continued social welfare support and general public willingness to continue to support policies for disabled people as just and reasonable. Equally, the corporate groups with a vested interest in the 'disability business' will strive to ensure that expenditure on disability policies expands.

Changing practices

From the late 1950s, segregated institutions attracted growing criticism, both from disabled people and their organizations and from mainstream providers, academics and politicians. In Britain, as in many other European and North American countries, inquiries documented the shortcomings in support and 'care' provided in old people's homes, psy-chiatric and 'mental handicap' hospitals (Townsend 1967; Martin 1985). Standards of residential care were very basic, with many examples of institutional abuse and harassment: 'There are staff who bully those who can't complain, who dictate what clothes people should wear, who switch the tele-vision off in the middle of a programme, and will take away "privileges" (like getting up for the day) when they choose' (Hunt 1966a: 154).

For Goffman (1961), the psychiatric asylum represented one form of 'total institution' characterized by long-term incarceration. Life within such institutions is strictly regimented and geared towards organizational goals. A strict demarcation line is drawn between the inmates and the staff, with mutually hostile and negative stereotypes characterizing their relations. On first entering the institution, inmates are subjected to various 'degradation' ceremonies amounting to a 'mortification of self'. The individual's former identity and clothes are removed, and replaced by an impersonal institutional identity (Humphries and Gordon 1992). Privacy is denied, and constant surveillance and regulation become standard routines.

British residential institutions studied by Eric Miller and Geraldine Gwynne (1972) in the 1960s confirmed this grim picture. They identified two contrasting value positions: one 'humanitarian' and the other 'liberal'. These correspond to distinctive styles of care: warehousing and horticultural. Humanitarian regimes stress maintaining life as long as possible, but in a minimalist, 'keep the residents cheerful' sense. In liberal regimes the goal is to attain 'normality', no matter how desperate the individual's circumstances (although the staff conception keeps inmates from expecting too much). Humanitarian approaches to warehousing regard the residents' lives as beyond improvement and akin to 'social death', so they are largely passive and dependent on care staff. By contrast, liberal horticulturalism stresses the potential for rehabilitation and satisfying an inmate's unmet needs. Miller and Gwynne (1972) expressed their preference for a positive regime of 'enlightened guardianship' that did not raise false expectations among residents about what can be achieved.

Nevertheless, there was a general shift in public policy in the second half of the twentieth century towards closing large, residential institutions. As a result, more disabled people were transferred to living 'in the community'. The number of places in British institutions registered under the Mental Deficiency Act of 1913 rose six-fold to 32,000 through the inter-war years. The association with social deviancy was such that having an illegitimate child might constitute grounds for confinement (Ryan with Thomas

1980). Large psychiatric institutions for the mentally ill demonstrated a similar trajectory in North America and many European countries. By 1955, the inmate population in county and state mental hospitals in the USA had risen to 558,000 (Conrad and Schneider 1980), but then a sharp decline occurred with the state mental hospital inmate population falling by 78 per cent by 1981. In Europe, the psychiatric hospital population was halved in Italy from 100,000 to 50,000 between 1968 and 1978, compared with a less dramatic decline in England and Wales from 148,000 in 1954 to fewer than 96,000 in the early 1980s.

The policy shift was thought a cheaper option by governments, and attractive for that reason alone. In addition, professional discourse argued that pharmacological innovations now enabled medical control of inmates outside the institution, while psychiatric professionals looked to greater integration with their medical counterparts (Scull 1984; Busfield 1986). The transition to living in the community was also accompanied by a reassertion of rehabilitation and caring goals by those working in the 'human care industries'. Yet, according to Wolf Wolfensberger, whatever the stated aims, their latent function has been to create and sustain large numbers of dependent and devalued people in order to secure employment for health and social care staff and profits for private companies. His review of the Dutch welfare system suggests that, instead of supporting independent living for 'people with learning difficulties', it actually 'discriminates against independence, communality, and non-congregate and non-institutional living' (Wolfensberger 1989: 37).

The search for alternative support for disabled people underpinned the introduction of 'normalization' policies. These emerged in Scandinavia in the late 1960s (Bank-Mikkelson 1980). The service goal was to decarcerate people with learning difficulties in long-stay institutions so as to enable them to lead more 'normal' lives by integrating them as far as possible into the mainstream. The philosophy and practice of normalization stressed the aim of assisting individuals into 'socially valued life conditions and socially valued roles' (Wolfensberger and Thomas 1983: 24). Yet critics have argued that normalization policies are professionally led in decisions about what constituted culturally valued and appropriate services (Brown and Smith 1992; Chappell 1992). Even policies invested with ideas of empowerment and anti-discrimination have been downplayed as an exercise of professional control by more subtle means (Chappell 1998; Stalker et al. 1999). This denotes the very thin line between enabling and disabling discourses and practices that applies more widely across such areas as counselling, advocacy and special needs education.

While the move away from living in large institutions continued, there was a corresponding growth in less formal, small-scale units and support networks (Russell 1998). However, these did not deliver the promised reworking of helper–helped relationships. Day centres and small group 'homes' or hostels 'in the community' still demonstrated an 'institutional' atmosphere (Barnes 1990), and concentrated on helping individuals cope with their personal tragedy.

Further criticism poured down on community care policies. The ideology of 'care' was castigated as integral to the individual approach to disability. Moreover, the overwhelming contribution is made by women, whether as informal carers in the family or friends or in the personal services. This attracted feminist charges that care policies were exploiting women's labour and time. Disabled feminists replied that this ignored the contribution of disabled women (in particular) as 'carers', besides portraying disabled people as a 'burden' or liable to exploit their children as unpaid helpers (Morris 1991). For disabled people, 'care' is the opposite of what they want from government policy or service providers, and misrepresents what people need to live 'independently' in the community. There has been a slow liberalization of social care policies, but there remains too little choice for disabled clients, and professional dominance of their needs and priorities is resistant to change.

There remains considerable debate regarding where care should be provided (in homes, institutions or something in between), who the providers of care should be, and what forms such 'care' might take (M. Barnes 1997). There have been renewed public campaigns, particularly from parents' groups, advocating the value of enlightened institutional regimes for some disabled children and adults. Yet, there has also been heightened policy support for service user 'participation' (Croft and Beresford 1992). The desired form and level of user involvement remain uncertain, but have demonstrated the existence of very different philosophies and strategies. On the one hand, there are user-led movements seeking autonomy, control and power, and on the other hand, there is an agency-led view of consulting with consumers about their preferences, in line with a market economy of welfare approach (see chapter 6).

Disabling professionals

In characteristic polemical vein, Ivan Illich (1977b) condemned the 'medicalization of life', and castigated medicine as 'a major threat to health' by misappropriating knowledge, mystifying its expertise, and creating a dependence on doctors, while ignoring medicine's deleterious consequences on individuals and society. 'I propose that we name the mid-twentieth century The Age of Disabling Professions, an age when people had "problems", experts had "solutions" and scientists measured imponderables such as "abilities" and "needs"' (Illich 1977a: 11). There is more than a hint of such criticism in the disability studies literature. Professionals are distinguished by their capacity and inclination to overcome lay opposition in deciding what is in the disabled person's 'best interests' (Gliedman and Roth 1980).

The link between the rise of professional dominance and institutional solutions to the 'problem' of disability has already been noted. With the moves towards decarceration in the second half of the twentieth century, there was a further transition in professional discourse. Attention now focused on a range of 'talking therapies', as a veritable 'psy complex' began to take root in advanced industrial societies (Ingleby 1983).

> Through self-inspection, self-problematisation, self-monitoring, and confession, we evaluate ourselves according to the criteria provided for use by others. Through self-reformation, therapy, techniques of body alteration, and the calculated reshaping of speech and emotion, we adjust ourselves by means of the techniques propounded by the experts of the soul. (Rose 1990: 10)

In addition, rehabilitation medicine occupied an even more prominent place in the lives of disabled people. It highlights the importance of taking the opportunities for a 'second chance' by working with appropriate professional experts. Eugenic thinking has also been revitalized by developments in biotechnology and genetic medicine. These raise the spectre that a 'new genetics' may stimulate a 'geneticization' of explanations of human behaviour and human values (Steinberg 1997).

There are examples where medical imperialism has not been successful and apparent opportunities for extension of professional interests have not been pursued. There are also instances of de-medicalization in which lay or State interests have pressed for medicalization in the face of a reluctant profession (Strong 1979). The enduring impression, however, is of the dominance of 'able-bodied' experts, particularly in the 'human service' professions (Wolfensberger 1989). Attempts to develop more enabling services have encountered considerable opposition from professionals and policy makers (Finkelstein and Stuart 1996). It is professional discourse on the 'special needs' of disabled people that prevails even over clearly expressed user 'demands' for support or 'quality of life' (Doyal and Gough 1991).

The enduring impression, from the perspective of disabled people, on both sides of the Atlantic (UPIAS 1976; DeJong 1979; Zola 1982), is that lay–professional relations are characterized as hierarchical, encouraging helplessness and dependence. They encapsulate the dependence and powerlessness of disabled people. Professionals are immersed in an individual approach, and regard disability as a health issue. The ideas, values and interests that permeate the helper–helped relationship are of 'able-bodied normalcy' (Finkelstein 1980: 17).

Review

Location on the wrong side of the 'oppression' divide characterizes the lives of disabled people from the more public through to the more personal domains. It is this combination of material disadvantages, powerlessness and demeaning cultural stereotyping that marks out disabled people's experience of social oppression. Their marginalization acquired a new intensity with the maturation of industrial capitalism, which also came to colonize disabled people's lives in new ways. Even where disabled people's support needs were identified, this led to renewed medicalization and control of their lives by charities and professionals in ways that continue to instil dependence and frustrate attempts to live more autonomous lives.

In summary, people with impairments have been 'isolated, incarcerated, observed, written about, operated on, instructed, implanted, regulated, treated, institutionalized, and controlled to a degree probably unequal to that experienced by any other minority group' (L. J. Davis 1997b: 1). The main beneficiaries are invariably represented as self-serving professionals, although their links with capitalism are not explored in detail. Again, attempts to link changes in the social oppression of disabled people with broader changes in productive forces, and in social and power relations remain unproved. At most, the impact of any changes is uncertain but probably uneven.

The next task is to turn from this broad socio-historical perspective to examine some of the empirical detail regarding contemporary patterns of social exclusion and oppression, including social divisions within the disabled population.

3

Social Oppression: Patterns and Social Divisions

A key aspect of most accounts of social oppression concerns the restrictions imposed on social groups such as disabled people which keep them from engaging in everyday social activities. To the extent that such social exclusion is practised, disabled people have fewer possibilities to advance and defend their interests within society. This provides corroborative evidence of their status as a subordinate group. In this chapter we begin by exploring contemporary patterns of social oppression. We focus on selected areas identified as important by disabled people: namely, education, income and employment, the built environment, leisure and 'right to life' issues. More specifically, is there evidence of exclusion across social life, and of uneven power relations between disabled and non-disabled people?

In the second half of the chapter, we examine how far there are lines of social division or difference in late twentieth- and early twenty-first-century society that have produced distinctive disparities within the disabled population. What is the interrelationship between disability and these other social divisions, such as gender, 'race' and social class, and how far does any impact fluctuate across the life course?

Social exclusion

Sociological studies of social exclusion traditionally focused on opportunities and outcomes in the paid labour market. This remains an important area, but needs to be supplemented by the incorporation of material from a much broader spread of social and economic life, such as right to life issues and the built environment, where arguably the interests of disabled people have been historically marginalized.

The focus spans material resources, including the ownership and control of the means of production, as well as access to political and civil rights, education, housing and what has been termed 'cultural capital' (Bourdieu 1973). The level and extent of social exclusion among disabled people are empirical questions, and liable to greater or lesser degrees of cross-national variation. However, available data are not always as comprehensive or detailed as required – certainly in comparison with other social divisions such as social class, gender and 'race'. Even more discomforting, most empirical surveys employ a medical definition of disability that takes functional limitation as the defining criterion.

Evidence of the form and extent of social participation rests on the ease of entry into, and subsequent level and type of involvement in, the areas selected for study. This suggests a number of key questions whereby to structure our discussion. Do barriers apply generally, or are they concentrated at specific points? How is participation restricted, by whom and on what (institutional or ideological) grounds? Are there key gatekeepers who facilitate participatory or, alternatively, orchestrate exclusionary practices? Are the processes overt and direct? Are these strategies directed at disabled people in general or targeted at (impairment-specific and other) subgroups? How far is the significance of the division between disabled and non-disabled people exacerbated or diminished across subgroups?

Education for all?

The expansion of formal education from a rich and privileged minority to the majority of children is associated with the maturation of industrial capitalist societies. The increasingly complex division of labour since the nineteenth century generated a growing need for an educated work-force with the full range of required economic skills and discipline. Formal education has concentrated on two main activities. First, schools act as socializing agencies, transmitting the dominant social rules, norms and values deemed appropriate for citizen regulation and participation. Second, they provide systems for channelling and selecting people for various social and employment roles (Marconis and Plummer 1997).

Today, 'special education' systems for disabled children are established around the world. The 'conventional' explanation is that segregated schools emerged as a philanthropic response to the 'special needs' of those unable to cope in the mainstream sector (Warnock 1978). An alternative 'conflict' perspective attributes their growth to the generalized interest in controlling potentially disruptive social problems, such as 'ineducable' or troublesome children (Oliver 1990). Subsequent trends have been shaped by power struggles between a range of vested professional interests, including doctors, educational psychologists and special education teachers (S. Tomlinson 1982).

Support for segregated provision comes from a variety of sources, including policy makers, professionals, parents and some sections of the disabled community. The prevailing argument has been that it is both more efficient and effective if expensive and scarce resources such as specialist teachers and equipment are concentrated in segregated school environments (Corbett 1998). In addition, mainstream schools are criticized for failing to satisfy a disabled child's educational, support and social needs. There is little meaningful inclusion in the classroom, curriculum or wider school activities. This is contrasted with the individualized support, more accessible environment and empathetic peer culture that special schools can provide (Barnes et al. 1999).

Segregated schooling has long been the preferred option of Deaf people and their organizations. Advocates maintain that it is the only way to ensure that they learn their own form of linguistic communication – sign language – and are socialized into the Deaf community, its history and culture, with a positive self-identity. Moreover, specialist schools are best qualified to disseminate the qualities and skills necessary to compete effectively in a predominantly aural society (Ladd 1988; Gregory and Hartley 1991). This has created a deep division between Deaf organizations and most other organizations of disabled people which believe that the special education system is deeply implicated in the oppression of people with impairments and should be abolished.

Critics of special education argue that removing disabled children from family, peers and the local community has wide-ranging negative effects (Morris 1997). Residential and segregated institutions restrict disabled children's opportunities to make friends with their non-disabled peers. Within the school, impairment issues often take priority. In addition, pupils experience a narrower curriculum due to lower expectations amongst policy makers, teachers and allied staff. Indeed, the educational attainment of disabled children in separate school environments is well below that of their non-disabled peers (Armstrong and Barton 1999).

In Britain, disabled children from 'special' schools leave with fewer qualifications and marketable skills than their non-disabled peers, so that working age disabled people are 'more than twice as likely on average than non-disabled people to have no formal qualifications' (Christie with Mensah-Coker 1999: 89). While Government documents proclaim their broad commitment to deliver 'excellence for all children' (DfEE 1997, 1998), the education system is geared increasingly to competition, choice and selection. Strategies include a national curriculum and published league tables with performance indicators of educational attainment and exam results (S. Tomlinson 1996). In this policy environment, disabled pupils are perceived as a liability.

Similar patterns of lower educational achievement among disabled children compared with their non-disabled peers exist around the world. In Canada and Australia, this is widely documented at both secondary and university levels (Chouinard 1997; Gleeson 1999). In the USA, disabled children are four times more likely than their non-disabled counterparts to have less than a ninth grade education (Charlton

1998: 45). Recent US federal policy has encouraged mainstreaming, with the proportion of children with an impairment spending at least 80 per cent of the school day being educated alongside children without an impairment rising from 30 to 40 per cent between 1988 and 1993. The percentage is much lower among those classified as 'mentally retarded' and with multiple impairments (Kaye 1997). Approximately 6 per cent of disabled children attend separate schools or facilities.

About 57 per cent of those labelled as having an impairment graduate from US high schools, although the figure varies significantly by impairment group. Achievement of a standard diploma is highest among those with a sensory impairment, but drops noticeably for those with a 'learning disabilities' label, who are most likely to receive a modified diploma or certificate of completion. Only about 15 per cent of disabled children on special education programmes continue into post-secondary education (Kaye 1997).

On the international stage, support for inclusive education has gathered momentum. As an illustration, the *Salamanca Statement and Framework for Action on Special Needs Education* was endorsed by 92 governments. It is unequivocal in declaring that 'the integration of children and youth with special needs is best achieved within inclusive schools that serve all children within a community' (UNESCO 1994: 11). However, translating this ambition into practical policies requires the development of a 'whole-school' policy that facilitates meaningful opportunities for children regardless of impairment. It depends on appropriate learning and teaching methods and skills, and not least on adequate resources and support (Armstrong and Barton 1999).

Employment and income

In most industrialized countries paid work is a significant criterion in categorizing people in terms of class, status and power. This means that people on the margins of the labour market encounter a variety of economic, political and social deprivations. This form of distributive injustice is widely experienced by disabled people (Barnes et al. 1999). Some have utilized the Marxist concept of a 'reserve army of labour' as amply illustrated by the ways in which disabled people are generally excluded from the work-force except where labour is in short supply, as in war-time or when the economy is 'booming' (Hyde 1996, 1998).

Unemployment rates vary over time and between countries, but they are routinely higher than the national average amongst adults with impairments. In 1995 two-thirds of disabled Americans of working age (11.4 million) were either not working or not seeking employment, with the unemployment rate for disabled people standing at 13.4 per cent, or more than twice the level for non-disabled Americans (LaPlante et al. 1996: 1). The figures for Australia tell a similar story. In 1993, the labour force participation rate for disabled people aged 15–64 stood at 46 per cent, compared with 63 per cent for the total population (Gleeson 1999). Comparable data for Britain indicate that almost 60 per cent of disabled people were classified as economically inactive in 1999 (Christie with Mensah-Coker 1999).

Disabled people are particularly under-represented in the professions and management, where there are higher earnings and greater job security and opportunities for promotion. Conversely, disabled people are over-represented in low-skilled, poorly paid, less secure jobs (Roulstone 1998). In Britain disabled men working full time earned on average 25 per cent less than their non-disabled counterparts, while the wages of disabled women were only two-thirds those of disabled men (Berthoud et al. 1993; Burchardt 2000b). In both Australia and Canada, disabled employees earn around 30 per cent less than their non-disabled equivalents (Gleeson 1999). Similarly, in the USA disabled workers earn only 64 per cent of the average non-disabled income, in large part due to lower hourly wages and fewer hours worked (LaPlante et al. 1996). Within the disabled population, those identified as people with learning difficulties or with a 'mental illness' experience much greater work disadvantages.

Besides this tendency towards vertical segregation, with disproportionate numbers of disabled people located in less skilled, lower-paid jobs with fewer promotion prospects, there is abundant evidence of horizontal segregation, with disabled people (or particular impairment groups) over-represented in specific occupations or congregated in sheltered workshops.

Since the mid-twentieth century, Western governments have tried various strategies to increase disabled people's participation in work. These include affirmative action programmes, employment quota schemes, designated employment and 'sheltered employment' sites. However, the demand for retrenchment in State intervention and expenditure has affected employment policies directed at disabled people (and others). Across North America and Europe there has been a heightened emphasis on training and 'Workfare' or 'New Deal' schemes to improve individuals' 'marketability'. In addition, anti-discrimination laws have been introduced to facilitate the recruitment and retention of disabled individuals in the work-place (see chapter 6). However, initiatives such as the 1990 Americans with Disabilities Act have brought little discernible improvement in labour market participation among disabled people (Kaye 1998).

The British experience offers abundant evidence of negative practices and attitudes to the employment of potential disabled people among both employers and non-disabled workers (Honey et al. 1993; Dench et al. 1996). Inaccessible transport and work-places and inflexible working conditions provide significant barriers. The increasing emphasis on formal qualifications, marketable skills, medical screening, and a 'socially acceptable' appearance by employers further contribute to the discrimination against groups within the disabled population. Similar patterns have been identified across Europe and North America (Thornton et al. 1997; Charlton 1998; NIDRR 2000).

A primary outcome of the exclusion of disabled people from the paid labour market is that the majority of disabled people experience higher levels of poverty and are more reliant on state welfare payments or charity for financial support – across Western countries (Martin and White 1988; Berthoud et al. 1993; Chouinard 1997). In Britain, state welfare benefits are the sole source of income for three-quarters of all disabled adults. Indeed, around 45 per cent of disabled Britons live below the official poverty line (Berthoud et al. 1993), while in the United States 30 per cent of disabled people of working age are classified as living in poverty. The rate is even higher amongst specific sections of the disabled community, rising to 72 per cent for disabled women with children under the age of six (LaPlante et al. 1996: 2). Moreover, individuals with an impairment have higher costs, simply because society is geared to the needs of non-disabled people. This is reinforced by expenditure on impairment-related items such as specialized equipment, personal clothing, heating, transport and housing adaptations.

As mentioned briefly in chapter 2, the claimed shift towards 'informationalization' puts a premium on highly educated and skilled workers, particularly in the rapidly developing and specializing new information technology sector, including self-employment opportunities (Castells 1996). Whereas an 'able body' has long been a prerequisite for inclusion in the work-force, now in the twenty-first century an 'able mind' may prove more significant (Cornes 1991). However, disabled people have historically had less access to technology, and currently demonstrate significantly lower ownership of computers or usage of the internet compared with the population as a whole (Kaye 2000).

It is also worth noting that social and economic inequalities are reflected in consumption of services. In countries with significant public and private welfare sectors, the reliance on public rather than private sector provision (in such areas as housing, transport and education) has been an important mark of social status. In practice, most disabled people remain disproportionately reliant on the state (and voluntary) sectors, while they are further differentiated as a result of their segregation in special schools and housing.

Built environment and transport

The quality of the built environment – housing, transport, buildings and public spaces – has a major impact on the extent and character of disabled people's exclusion from mainstream society (see box 3.1). Indeed, the institutional discrimination against disabled people is perhaps nowhere so apparent as in the built environment (Barnes 1991).

Box 3.1   Examples of exclusion

- physical barriers to movement for disabled people, including broken surfaces on thoroughfares (streets, guttering, paving) which reduce or annul the effectiveness of mobility aids (e.g. wheelchairs, walking frames)
- building architecture which excludes the entry of anyone unable to use stairs and hand-operated doors
- public and private transport modes which assume that drivers and passengers are non-impaired
- public information (e.g. signage) presented in forms that assume a common level of visual and aural ability (Gleeson 1999: 137)

Traditionally, urban infrastructures have been designed with little if any thought for the needs of people with impairments (Hahn 1986; Andrew Walker 1995; Imrie 1996). An inaccessible built environment has a knock-on effect for a wide range of activities, including the choice about where and when to work, type and location of housing, and participation in leisure activities. This in turn inhibits earning and shopping opportunities, while also often leading to higher travel costs and investment of more time in making the necessary or alternative arrangements.

Although most Western societies now have some form of legislative framework whereby to address inaccessible built environments, these policies have been slow to make an impression on discriminatory urban design. In Britain, for example, the 1970 Chronically Sick and Disabled Persons Act instructed local authorities to address the access needs of disabled people with reference to housing, public buildings, schools and universities. In the 1970s local authorities' 'completions' of wheelchair-adaptable dwellings (houses where people can live with the minimum of assistance) rose substantially, but thereafter declined dramatically to a handful in the 1990s (Harris et al. 1997).

Moreover, despite the rhetoric of 'social inclusion' that pervades recent official publications, segregated 'special needs' housing remains central to Government plans for 'community care'. Even so, many of these properties do not satisfy disabled people's requirements. For example, too few have more than one bedroom, even though most disabled people live with their families, and a significant minority of single disabled people need two-bedroom housing to accommodate a personal assistant. Given the shortages identified, a more cost-effective alternative would be to build new accessible housing rather than adapt existing properties. The preferred option is 'universal design' or 'lifetime homes'. These are designed to satisfy the changing needs of householders, and can accommodate young and old, disabled and non-disabled (Rowe 1990).

The specific circumstances surrounding the decarceration of people in asylums illustrate how these groups of disabled people are left to fend for themselves within an often hostile urban environment. North American studies document how inadequate public funding and resources, as well as some community opposition, has rendered many former inmates dependent on welfare and social service support (Dear and Wolch 1987; Wolch and Dear 1989). In Britain, homelessness among the disabled population is relatively high, particularly among mental health system 'survivors' (Sayce 2000).

Inaccessible public transport systems also provide major barriers to social and economic participation. Unfortunately, among the most commonly used forms, buses, trains, coaches and planes have not been developed with disabled customers in mind. Indeed, with the relatively high cost of purchasing and running a car, access to other forms of transport is even more crucial.

Even allowing for some recent significant innovations, transportation systems generally present considerable accessibility barriers to disabled people. Nevertheless, some tangible improvements have been made. In the USA, public transport has become noticeably more accessible – at least to those with mobility and sensory impairments – in the last quarter of the twentieth century. The introduction of low-floor buses and new technologies such as digitized speech announcements has had a discernible impact. Public opinion polls report that three-quarters of disabled people perceive an improvement in the accessibility of the built environment since the passage of the Americans with Disabilities Act (ADA).

Nevertheless, significant barriers remain in such areas as air travel, inter-city coaches and the New York subway system (Kaye 1998). For example, the ADA decrees that new inter-city buses and a minimum number of 'key' railway stations should be accessible, but progress has been slow. In the mid-1990s, fewer than 25 per cent of Chicago's rail stations were accessible, while the situation in Boston, New York and Philadelphia was 'even worse' (Charlton 1998: 106). A bleak picture is painted of disabled city dwellers 'often trapped in restrictive living units and . . . unable to gain access to a city's resources by transportation systems not adapted for them' (Gilderbloom and Rosentraub (1990: 271).

One difficulty has been the heterogeneity of the disabled population, which militates against easy 'universal design' solutions. Dropped kerbs favoured by wheelchair users can be a hazard to people with visual impairments. Mobile disabled people may require a narrow toilet compartment with rails securely fixed at either side with walls to lean against for support, whereas wheelchair users typically need more space to manoeuvre. The two groups also have different preferences for the location of entry phones. The task of designing a universal physical environment remains the goal, if not yet close to being a feasible proposition. Even where built environments have been made more accessible, there remain difficulties and 'concerns about aesthetics, privacy, sociability and comfort' (Marks 2000: 52).

Leisure

There is a considerable literature emphasizing the significance that leisure has assumed in everyday lives in late capitalist societies. In Western societies, with society and culture increasingly geared to consumption, leisure has become big business, just as people's self-identities are increasingly geared to consumption activities (A. Tomlinson 1990). Certainly in terms of the acquisition of valued consumer goods, disabled people, who usually have lower than average incomes, generally lose out.

Although popularly perceived as equivalent to 'free time', leisure choices are widely constrained and socially patterned.

How we use our leisure time has become a key marker in terms of social identity, status and life-style. Leisure is also a key arena for developing personal and sexual relationships. 'It is in the sphere of consumption – conspicuous leisure on the basis of adequate disposable income – that many will seek to express their sense of freedom, their personal power, their status and aspiration' (A. Tomlinson 1990: 6). Contrary to popular belief, many disabled people have less leisure time than non-disabled contemporaries. One explanation is that essential domestic and personal activities take longer to complete; in addition, disabled people frequently experience problems allocating time between their own personal needs, work and leisure pursuits.

People's ability to enjoy leisure time is closely related to their employment status. Not being in paid employment typically reduces those social contacts and friendship networks that sustain many leisure activities. Again, while disabled people are able to obtain vital equipment such as electric wheelchairs and reading aids to overcome disability in employment from statutory authorities, governments do not provide equivalent support for leisure activity. As a result, disabled people with below-average disposable income have far fewer leisure choices (Martin and White 1988; Martin et al. 1989).

The home occupies centre stage for leisure activities, such as watching television and videos, visiting or entertaining friends, listening to the radio and CDs, and reading (CSO 2000). Needless to say, each of these presents specific barriers for some groups within the disabled community, such as those with visual and hearing impairments. Leisure activities outside the home are severely hampered by an inaccessible transport system and built environment. Transport systems such as trains, buses, coaches and taxis all present some form of barrier to disabled people, so this increases dependence on others for travel.

There is also considerable public and private corporate apprehension about involving disabled people in mainstream leisure activities. A regular complaint is that places of entertainment such as cinemas and theatres have used safety and fire regulations to exclude disabled people with mobility, sensory and communication impairments or to demand that they be accompanied by an 'able-bodied' person (Barnes 1991). Wheelchair users are often urged to telephone first, 'to be sure of getting in'. Choice and spontaneity are thereby restricted.

Social hostility towards disabled people has led to the development of segregated leisure activities. In Britain, they include day centres, adult training centres and social clubs. These are particularly targeted at younger and older disabled people, and span a number of basic recreational and social activities. They tend to reinforce traditional ideologies of care towards disabled people because of their institutional atmosphere and separation from mainstream facilities.

Despite improvements in the built environment since the 1980s, disabled people demonstrate high levels of social isolation. US data indicate that they are twice as likely (at 20 per cent) to live alone, and that they express higher levels of dissatisfaction with their social lives, with less contact with friends, neighbours and relatives than non-disabled people. As many as 58 per cent had not been to a cinema in the previous year, two-thirds go out to a restaurant less than once a week, and even fewer attend church. Three-quarters had not attended a live music performance, and over two-thirds had not attended a sporting event (compared with 43 per cent of non-disabled people). Only 56 per cent of disabled people go food shopping at least once a week, compared to 85 per cent of non-disabled Americans (Kaye 1998).

Surveys of disabled people's expressed satisfaction with their social lives reveal higher levels of dissatisfaction among the younger age groups. This is because young people generally are far more concerned with peer group relationships and life-style pursuits, and are relatively more reliant upon activities outside the home for social contacts. Elizabeth Anderson's and Lynda Clarke's study *Disability in Adolescence* (1982) compared the social lives of disabled and non-disabled youngsters between fourteen and eighteen years old. The disabled children led a more solitary existence, and if they did go outside the home for leisure, it was mainly restricted to outings with family members. The isolation was most acute among disabled children who had attended special schools. The majority of this group interacted only with other young people with impairments. Furthermore, some research studies suggest that people who acquire impairments often experience acute feelings of isolation as they lose contact with non-disabled friends and experience a sharp reduction in their choice of leisure activities (Morris 1989).

Leisure activities also overlap with personal and intimate relationships. Historically, there has been a 'special concern, which often verged on obsession, with segregating the sexes in institutions for disabled people' (Humphries and Gordon 1992: 100). Its generalization outside institutions has led to frequent criticism that disabled people are constrained from exploring opportunities to express their sexuality, including same sex relations (Finger 1992; Shakespeare et al. 1996; Gillespie-Sells et al. 1998). Studies of disabled people's sexuality, or 'untold desires' (Shakespeare et al. 1996), provide illuminating narrative accounts of neglected issues of 'sexuality, relationships, and personal identity' (p. 5):

> Sexuality is often the source of our deepest oppression; it is also often the source of our deepest pain. It's easier for us to talk about – and formulate strategies for changing – discrimination in employment, education, and housing than to talk about our exclusion from sexuality and reproduction. (Finger 1992: 9)

The cultural representation of disabled people has often stressed their lack of sexual attractiveness (Gartner and Joe 1987; Thomson 1997). Cultural stereotypes, the general societal and professional antagonism towards disabled people having sexual partners or children, and beliefs that sexual activity is solely about sexual intercourse, provide further restrictions on the 'leisure pursuits' of disabled people.

'Right to life' issues

Disabled people have increasingly argued that their oppression and reduced participation in society are highlighted in debates around contentious social and ethical issues such as abortion, euthanasia, violence and abuse. These have all thrown into sharp relief public estimates of their value as human beings. For example, violence and abuse (emotional, sexual and physical) are significantly and systematically directed at disabled people as a group (Chenoweth 1999). It is a particular feature of the lives of disabled children and women in institutions (Westcott and Cross 1996; Rioux et al. 1997; Stanley et al. 1999). Sweden sterilized 60,000 women between 1935 and 1976, including many with learning difficulties. Similar eugenic-inspired laws to permit sterilization and abortion were passed in Finland, Denmark, Switzerland and Japan. Yet these policies have been widely overlooked on the grounds that disabled people's lives are of lesser value, or in some instances are considered not worth living (Sobsey 1994).

Across the world, campaigns over recent decades to legalize abortion have raised particular fears among many disabled people. As an illustration, Britain's 1967 Abortion Act states that 'a pregnancy may be lawfully terminated' if it threatens the health of the pregnant woman or if there is 'substantial risk' that if the child is born 'it would suffer from such physical and mental abnormalities as to be seriously handicapped'. Importantly, advances in medical technology, including amniocentesis and ultrasound scanning, have greatly increased doctors' ability to detect perceived impairment in the unborn child.

Women are often put under enormous pressure to abort a pregnancy once an impairment is identified – both by professionals and by their families (Rock 1996; C. Thomas 1997). The typical justification is that a disabled infant places an emotional and financial 'burden' on the child's family and society as a whole. In practice, most disabled children are born to parents with little or no experience of disability, who have assimilated a personal tragedy approach. Little attention has been given to identifying ways of supporting families with disabled children. Additionally, many disabled people claim that selective abortion on impairment grounds devalues their existence and undermines their demands for equal rights and opportunities.

Discussions around the legalization of euthanasia similarly pose a direct threat to disabled people. Former Colorado governor Richard Lamm argued that terminally ill and disabled people had a 'duty to die' (quoted in Russell 1998: 29). While the medical profession has been formally opposed to 'mercy killing', in cases where there is agreement that the quality of life is unacceptable, a person's life may be terminated with medical approval, perhaps after prior discussion with the patient or the family. Critics argue that, once legalized (as now in the Netherlands), there will be growing social pressure on people with impairments to opt for euthanasia.

This runs parallel with claims that disabled people are sometimes denied equal health and social care treatment (A. Davis 1989). The production of 'quality of life' scales or measures for calculating the potential impact of medical interventions has exacerbated this foreboding. The understandable fear of disabled people is that they will be singled out as undeserving cases for costly, life-saving medical intervention (*Disability Tribune* 2000).

Thus far the discussion has concentrated on the social exclusion of disabled people as a group, as compared with their non-disabled counterparts, but the consistent patterns of lower social participation by disabled people raise the question of the extent to which these restrictions are experienced evenly across the disabled population.

Social divisions

Given the consistent patterns of marginalization identified here, it is extraordinary that so few social scientists have been moved to argue that 'disability must be considered as a factor contributing to the production and distribution of stratification in its own right' (Jenkins 1991: 557). However, the polarization of disabled and non-disabled populations has attracted growing criticism for portraying a 'false universalism'. The initial concentration on disability as a 'master status' that effectively submerges the impact of other social divisions has become widely contested. The presumed homogeneity of disabled people's experience of exclusion has been countered by demands that studies incorporate the interaction of disability with gender (Deegan and Brooks 1985; Fine and Asch 1988; Wendell 1989, 1996; Morris 1991), 'race' and ethnicity (Stuart 1993; Begum et al. 1994), sexuality

(Shakespeare et al. 1996; Gillespie-Sells et al. 1998), age (Zarb and Oliver 1992; Priestley 2000) and social class (Jenkins 1991).

However, a simple additive approach encourages the construction of a misleading league table of oppressions encountered by different subgroups of disabled people. As Nasa Begum argues, the 'double oppression' of being a disabled woman, for example, yields to the 'triple oppression of being a black disabled woman (who experiences) . . . racism, sexism and handicapism' (1992: 70–1). In practice, these dimensions are interlocking and provide a complex experience of 'simultaneous' rather than separate oppressions. It is not possible to 'simply prioritise one aspect of our oppression to the exclusion of others' (Begum 1994: 35). However, it has proved to be much easier to identify simultaneous oppression and associated responses in theory rather than in practice.

Gender and disability

Some of the earliest attempts to address the experience of disability focused on its impact on women. In two collections edited by Jo Campling (1979, 1981), the contributors draw attention to the problems faced by disabled women in such key areas as personal relationships, sexuality, motherhood, education and employment, and media stereotypes.

However, early theorization of the gendered experience of disability is at the heart of studies developed by Michelle Fine and Adrianne Asch (1981, 1988). In their analyses of the American literature, they argue disabled men have had relatively more opportunities to oppose the stigma associated with impairment and thus to strive to achieve typical male roles. By contrast, '[e]xempted from the "male" productive role and the "female" nurturing one, having the glory of neither, disabled women are arguably doubly oppressed' (Asch and Fine 1988: 13). Most recently, attempts have been made to recognize a wider set of differences among disabled women, not least on the bases of 'race' (Begum 1992; Vernon 1999), sexuality (Tremain 1996) and age.

Empirical evidence from the USA and Britain confirms the significant degree of social exclusion encountered by disabled women in the labour market (Fine and Asch 1988; Lonsdale 1990). Thus, disabled women experience disadvantages that set them apart from both disabled men and non-disabled women – economically, socially and psychologically. As a consequence, disabled women are either ignored in feminist analyses or portrayed as passive victims: 'Perceiving disabled women as childlike, helpless, and victimized, non-disabled feminists have severed them from the sisterhood in an effort to advance more powerful, competent, and appealing female icons' (Asch and Fine 1988: 4).

In *Pride Against Prejudice*, Jenny Morris (1991) is equally critical of feminism for its failure to address the experiences of disabled women. While it has fought long and hard to challenge society's rigid gender roles, it has embraced the personal tragedy representation of disabled women as incapable of performing 'normal' female roles. From the perspective of disabled women, 'we are prescribed a life of passive dependence. Our neutered sexuality, negative body-image and restricted gender roles are a direct consequence of the processes and procedures which shape the lives of women' (Begum 1992: 81). Disabled women have also been discouraged from becoming mothers on various grounds that often exaggerate risks, or deny choice, such as perceived threats to their own health, passing on an impairment to their children, or their supposed incapacity to be 'good mother[s]' (Finger 1991; C. Thomas 1997).

Nevertheless, the feminist rallying call that the 'personal is political' has been enthusiastically and easily incorporated into disabled women's writings. This stresses that 'women's everyday reality is informed and shaped by politics and is necessarily political' (hooks 1984: 24). It has triggered a growing literature on individual disabled women's stories of living with impairment (Campling 1981; Browne et al. 1985; Deegan and Brooks 1985; Driedger and Gray 1992). This literature consciously set out to overcome what was regarded as an overwhelming focus on disabled men's experiences, such as at work or their sexual concerns, while female sexuality, reproduction and child rearing were largely ignored. To politicize the personal domain means taking control, 'including the negative parts to the experience' (Morris 1993a: 69).

'Race' and disability

'Race', or ethnicity, also plays an important part in social and economic positioning – for both disabled and non-disabled people. A similar impact is evident in media representations. It has been argued that a black disabled identity can be understood only within the context of a deeply embedded social exclusion of black people – that is, 'institutional racism' (Confederation of Indian Organizations 1987). The extent of this oppression means that black disabled people form 'a discrete minority within a minority', and often face 'exclusion and marginalisation even within disabled communities and the disability movement' (Hill 1994: 74).

Studies of the interaction between different social divisions and processes provide a picture of 'double' or 'multiple' oppression (Baxter et al. 1990), although Ossie Stuart (1993) argues that 'being a black disabled person is not a "double" experience, but a single one grounded in British racism' (p. 99). He contends that the distinctiveness of black disabled people's oppression is threefold: 'first, limited or no individuality and identity; second, resource discrimination; finally, isolation within black communities and the family' (p. 95).

In Britain, racism is not so much located in 'colour' but widened to cultural difference, so that black disabled people are distanced from both anti-racists and the disabled people's movement. This is evident in the absence of black people in disabled people's organizations, and suggests the need to build a 'distinct and separate black disabled identity' (p. 94). Yet black disabled people are also marginalized within the black community because of their exclusion from employment and leisure activities and their 'inability to attain accepted roles within black communities' (p. 99). It follows that other minorities within the black disabled community experience further 'unique' forms of simultaneous oppression.

Studies demonstrate the ways in which 'race' affects how disabled people are treated in education and work. This leads, according to Nasa Begum, to complex survival strategies and alliances between black disabled people and other oppressed groups. Specific aspects will be prioritized according to the context. Sometimes black disabled people form alliances with other disabled people to challenge disability, while on other occasions they unite with other black people to fight racism. 'The very nature of simultaneous oppression means that as Black Disabled men and women, and Black Disabled lesbians and gay men we cannot identify a single source of oppression to reflect the reality of our lives' (Begum 1994: 35). It is not possible to 'simply prioritise one aspect of our oppression to the exclusion of others' (p. 35). Yet the notion of 'multiple oppression' is misleading, because it separates the many different dimensions of inequality, as if these can be compartmentalized in everyday experience and then added together in an overall balance sheet.

In summary, these studies demonstrate the importance of analysing the complex interplay of oppressions in ways that avoid a simplistic oppressor–oppressed divide and allow scope for agency or resistance:

> The significance of such a model is that, first, it poses a dynamic relationship between the individual, power and structure, its multifacets or many mirrors reflect the fact that social divisions impact on people, singly or in groups in different ways, at different times, in different situations. At one or many moments, in one or many places issues of disability may be highlighted; at another moment the inequalities of class may predominate for the same person or group. (F. Williams 1992: 214–15)

This focus on the interrelationship of different (simultaneous) lines of oppression exposes the internal fault lines, but still leaves open how exclusionary processes operate across social contexts. As Barbara Fawcett argues, a middle-class, white, disabled man challenging a restaurant's lack of accessibility may appear very powerful to a black, non-disabled waitress. Conversely, the same waitress may demand that a white man with learning difficulties leave the restaurant because his table manners are upsetting non-disabled customers (Fawcett 2000: 52–3). 'The challenge then becomes to recognise and challenge oppression, whilst fully acknowledging complexity and interrelational elements' (Fawcett 2000: 53).

Life cycle influences

The notion of a normative life course (childhood, adulthood and old age) has been a key discursive claim within social policy. Its central stages, statuses and transitions are institutionally and culturally produced. Central institutions such as the family, economy and education exercise potentially defining roles. Traditionally in industrial societies, social class was a defining force in people's lives, but its grip has been loosened, creating less certainty in individual or family biographies. This leads to more life-planning and self-monitoring, as well as greater fears of risk or failure and conflicting institutional demands (Beck 1992).

What, then, is the consequence of superimposing impairment/disability on these life cycle patterns? It is widely accepted that it is important to identify the point in the life cycle when the impairment was acquired. Researchers have identified three main trajectories, or 'disability careers': first, people whose impairment is diagnosed at birth or in early childhood; second, those who acquire an impairment during the adolescent or early adult years, often as a result of an illness or injury; and third, older people whose impairment is most often attributed to the ageing process (Jenkins 1991).

People born with a congenital condition or who acquire an impairment very early in life experience unrelenting socialization to low expectations or an 'abnormal' life-style, while few positive role models exist to demonstrate a contrary picture. Moreover, families and special schools may hide children with a congenital impairment to protect them from discrimination, perhaps until early adolescence. The majority of disabled children grow up in households and communities where there is no other disabled person. A variety of factors, including the actions of parents and close family members, lengthy periods of hospitalization, segregated special education, and a largely inaccessible physical environment, ensure that many of these children assume a conventional 'disabled identity'. Indeed, many of those growing up with an impairment are shielded from the full impact of disablement until they try to participate in mainstream leisure activities or look for work (Anderson and Clarke 1982; Thomas, Bax and Smythe 1989; Hirst and Baldwin 1995). Nevertheless, in a comparison of disabled and non-disabled young people, the former reported lower job aspirations, poor or non-existent careers advice, employer discrimination or disinterest, and marginalization in the labour market (Alan Walker 1982). This also links with evidence that key transition indicators, such as age when leaving home, getting married, becoming a parent, and entry into the labour force occur later among disabled compared with non-disabled people (Priestley 2000).

Another scenario awaits individuals who acquire an impairment in later life. Some are forced into a sudden and substantial re-evaluation of their identity, perhaps reinforced within a short time period by downward economic and social mobility. The demands of manual work may lead to some movement into non-manual occupations. Mildred Blaxter (1976) notes how this group demonstrates either 'discontinuity', with a sharp transfer into unemployment, or 'drift', that refers to a more gradual process of downward mobility. Locker's (1983) study of people with rheumatoid arthritis identifies similar patterns. For other writers, the development of impairment as a result of a 'chronic illness', rather than an accident, is more gradual and therefore less dramatic in its threat to self-identity (Safilios-Rothschild 1970).

A key factor is that those individuals who acquire an impairment in middle age are much more likely to have assimilated a traditional 'personal tragedy' approach to disability, so the 'shock' of their impairment can prove particularly traumatic (Oliver and Barnes 1998; Burchardt 2000a). In comparison, people whose impairment is associated more with the ageing process may interpret their experiences, as do significant others around them, whether family or service providers, as seemingly inevitable 'facts of life' and so 'normalize' their condition (Priestley 2000).

Review

The pattern of social participation, or lack of it, experienced by disabled people demonstrates that exclusionary barriers remain deeply embedded in the structures and processes of contemporary societies. The under-participation in paid employment has obvious material consequences, but is further reinforced by lower levels of educational attainment, lack of accessibility in the built environment, and restricted leisure opportunities. Irrespective of where the spotlight has been directed in this discussion, disabled people, compared with their non-disabled counterparts, show a clear pattern of restricted life chances, choices and opportunities for social participation.

At the same time, there is ample evidence that the extent and form of exclusion demonstrated also reflect the interaction of disability with other sources of oppression, such as 'race', gender and age. However, there remains very little research evidence on other key divisions such as social class and sexuality, or the effects of interaction between these categories.

Thus far our focus has been on disability as a form of social oppression. Issues of impairment have been largely set aside. Nevertheless, the separation of impairment from studies of disability remains a bone of contention. The calls to 'bring impairment back in' provide the trailer for chapter 4.

4
Impairment, Disability and the Body

The polarization of impairment and disability has been the linchpin of claims surrounding a social model of disability. From this 'fundamentalist' perspective, a focus on impairment and associated experiences risks undermining the social model's political project (Oliver 1990, 1996a). Yet recently there have been calls from 'revisionists' to 'bring impairment back in'. The merits of doing so have been strongly disputed, and highlight the diverse theoretical and political standpoints now contained within the disability studies literature. We will examine this continuing exchange in the first part of the chapter, with specific reference to the development of a social theory of impairment, including the thorny issue of disentangling 'impairment effects' (C. Thomas 1999).

These debates have developed a particular focus on experience. This provides an immediate overlap with the considerable sociological literature on 'chronic illness and disability' that is examined in the second part of the chapter. It has been a particular target for social model advocates, primarily because it is securely encamped within an individual, medicalized approach to disability. A further aspect to this discussion is the burgeoning social theory interest in difference and the development of multiple identities. This reinforces the concern with prioritizing people's feelings and experiences, rather than structural factors and the social construction of identity, including the experiences and identities of disabled people.

Finally, we explore the recent impact on disability studies of recent theorizing of the body. Much of the inspiration has been derived from Foucauldian analyses of the 'disabled body'. This has produced new alliances and divisions, with some sociologists and a growing number of contributors to disability studies taking the post-structuralist/post-modernist path. This, in turn, has generated what we regard as a more compelling, eclectic approach that draws on interpretative (phenomenological), social-constructionist and materialist insights.

Separating impairment and disability

The separation of impairment and disability characterizes schemes advanced by both UPIAS (see chapter 1) and Disabled People's International (DPI) (box 4.1).

Box 4.1   DPI definitions of impairment and disability

- **Impairment**: 'the functional limitation within the individual caused by physical, mental or sensory impairment'.
- **Disability**: 'the loss or limitation of opportunities to take part in the normal life of the community on an equal level with others due to physical and social barriers'. (DPI 1982)

In these definitions, impairment refers to bio-physiological limitations or 'defects' as determined by medical or equivalent professional experts. However, the presence of an impairment does not mean automatic transfer to the status of a disabled person. It becomes an issue at the point where social barriers exclude that individual from participation in everyday life activities, although in practice this still leaves scope for considerable uncertainty. One obvious question is whether disease or sickness, such as HIV/AIDS, cancer or diabetes, are considered impairments? The UPIAS definition suggests a more open door than the DPI focus on functional limitations.

From a sociological viewpoint, impairment, like illness, is analysed as a social construction, in that its meaning and the responses to it are historically and culturally specific. Medical knowledge has been continuously augmented by the 'discovery' of new impairments, although there has also been public pressure to give a medical label to some conditions, as with myalgic encephalomyelitis (ME). A further complexity is introduced where administrative definitions diverge from medical as well as lay understandings.

In practice, there has been little debate in the disability studies literature about the formulation of impairment in terms of biomedical characteristics. Instead, attention has been devoted to pressing forward with the analysis of disability as a social construction or creation. One of the key architects of social model theorizing explains the separation of impairment and disability as primarily a 'pragmatic attempt to identify and address issues that can be changed through collective action rather than medical or other professional treatment' (Oliver 1996b: 38). The political radicalism of disability theory was built (in Britain anyway) on a resistance to theorizing (or even discussing) impairment. 'The achievement of the disability movement has been to break the link between our bodies and our social situation and to focus on the real cause of disability, i.e. discrimination and prejudice' (Shakespeare 1992: 40).

In this vein, most early (male) interpreters of the social model dismissed 'what it feels like' knowledge as a 'discredited and sterile approach to understanding and changing the world', precisely because it rested on individual impairment issues (Finkelstein 1996: 34). A division was identified between those who concentrate on challenging disabling social barriers ('outside in') and those who want to explore the attitudes and emotions associated with the personal experience of impairment and disability ('inside out'). Finkelstein (1996) further proposed that this division relates to 'active' and 'passive' approaches to disability politics.

Nevertheless, since the late 1980s, a growing number of disability writers have resisted such denunciations and challenged early social model approaches for concentrating exclusively on structural barriers (and access to material resources) and disregarding the cultural and experiential aspects of disablism. There are three main strands to this particular critique.

First, there has been criticism of social model accounts for overlooking the 'oppressive' aspects of impairment. Comments such as 'disablement has nothing to do with the body' (Oliver 1996b: 41–2) are vehemently rejected on the grounds that the 'experiences of our bodies *can* be unpleasant or difficult' (Crow 1996: 58), as with the physical pain, cognitive distress and uncertainty associated with conditions such as rheumatoid arthritis and multiple sclerosis. Or, in Susan Wendell's words, it is necessary to understand what it means for an individual to 'live with the suffering body, with that which cannot be noticed without pain, and that which cannot be celebrated without ambivalence' (Wendell 1996: 179).

Hence, any attempt to uncouple impairment from disability contradicts an individual's everyday experiences (French 1993). Similar viewpoints are expressed in American, Canadian and European anthologies of disabled women's experiences (Campling 1981; Brown et al. 1985; Deegan and Brooks 1985; Driedger and Gray 1992). Indeed, disabled feminists took the lead in challenging the disregard of impairment in socio-political approaches. For Jenny Morris,

> there is a tendency within the social model of disability to deny the experience of our bodies, insisting that our physical differences and restrictions are *entirely* socially created. While environmental barriers and social attitudes are a crucial part of our experience of disability – and do indeed disable us – to suggest that this is all there is to it is to deny the personal experience of physical and intellectual restrictions, of illness, of the fear of dying. (Morris 1991: 10)

From this standpoint, the experience of disability and impairment 'meld together in a holistic fashion' (C. Thomas 1999: 43). This tallies with claims by medical sociologists that a significant element of the 'oppressive quality of chronic illness and disability' is for many people 'undeniably to do with the pain and discomfort of bodies' (G. Williams 1998: 243). It also fits with a wider explanation, that the preoccupation with the personal experience of impairment has been encouraged by a more 'confessional' late modern culture.

Second, there are counter-claims that specific impairment groups are marginalized by social model writings. The most frequently mentioned candidates include people with learning difficulties (Chappell 1992; Corbett 1998; Goodley 2000), Deaf people (Corker 1993, 1998a), and those with the label of 'mental illness' (Beresford 2000; Mulvany 2000; Sayce 2000). The status of the 'impairment' category that underpins the social model of disability is much more contested and flexible than original formulations suggested or allowed. For example, people who describe themselves as 'mental health system survivors' argue forcefully that their difference (or 'distress') is not properly or helpfully categorized as an impairment. Again, many Deaf people identify as a linguistic minority, and reject their impairment status and designation as part of the disabled population.

'Fundamentalist' writers have demonstrated a willingness to accept the contested epistemological standing of some medical labels, such as 'mental illness' and 'learning difficulties'. Indeed, the changing and expanding labels attached to people now designated as having 'learning difficulties' reinforce claims of the socially constructed basis of the impairment category. However, there has been an uneasy stand-off with those Deaf people who claim a linguistic rather than an impairment status. Attempts to include people with other long-standing illnesses and conditions raise similar theoretical and political dilemmas: 'Can a fat woman call herself disabled' (Cooper 1997).

The experience of people with the label of 'learning difficulties' demonstrates a further dimension to the critique of the social model. There has been increasing criticism that it represents a damning indictment of their basic humanity, not simply a statement of their functional limitations: 'hence, this group's insistence on being perceived as *people first*' (Gillman et al. 1997: 690). Few question the extent of their devaluation in 'a society which defines and confines all meaning and worth in terms of production, profit, and pervasive greed' (Trent 1994: 277). Yet the focus on breaking down disabling social and environmental barriers has been slower to benefit people with learning difficulties than other impairment groups (Ferguson 1994; Walmsley 1997). In practice, the social model sits more easily with a liberal argument that assumes a type of independence, rationality and self-sufficiency that some people who have others to 'speak for' them cannot always command (Kittay 2001: 559).

Overall, the disability studies literature contains little discussion of the social construction of medical knowledge about impairment beyond labelling approaches. This has been particularly explored with respect to 'mental illness' and 'mental handicap', but has also attracted much attention as 'new' conditions strive for 'impairment' status, even where their disabling consequences may be accepted, such as ME. In the sociological tradition, social constructionism refers to the critical analysis of common-sense, taken-for-granted knowledge, beliefs and practices and an insistence that knowledge claims be located within specific historical, cultural and social time periods (Burr 1995). Hence the production (and discovery) of knowledge is an inherently social process. However, the arrival of post-structuralism/post-modernism moved these debates on to new terrain, where the focus is on competing discourses and how these position social groups (Foucault 1980). From this perspective, the main issue is how impairment is constituted at the discursive level (without presuming any necessary relationship to a specific body-mind condition) (Fawcett 2000).

Third, critics of the social model charge that it has tended to downplay the potential for considerable variation in the experience of both impairment and disability across the disabled population. The person with cerebral palsy, for example, has a different experiential vantage point from that of a person with a hearing impairment or someone with the label of mental illness (French 1993; Booth and Booth 1998; C. Thomas 1999). Social model accounts have been specifically criticized for excluding those groups for whom language and communication exert an independent effect in mediating oppression and exclusion (Corker 1998a).

This links with a growing interest in late twentieth-century social theory in 'flexible', 'multiple' and 'contested' identities. It further encourages attention to the significance of experiential divisions within the disabled population, for example, on the basis of gender and sexuality. Thus, it has been argued that the treatment of disabled lesbians exposes 'the white heterosexualism that dominates the disability rights movement, a movement which seldom aligns itself with queer struggles for justice in the institutional, symbolic-discursive, and social realms' (Tremain 1996: 21).

Each of these criticisms has attracted considerable debate. The issues raised around experience have been addressed and elaborated in sociological approaches both interpretative and post-structuralist. Contributions from the latter camp have also been instrumental in exploring the social construction of impairment. Yet, before reviewing these debates in more detail, it is important to summarize claims about the social model and 'impairment effects'.

Carol Thomas has recently sought to clarify the considerable confusion triggered by contrasting interpretations of a 'social model' approach to impairment and disability:

> *Disability is about restrictions of activity which are socially caused. That is, disability is entirely socially caused. But some restrictions of activity are caused by illness and impairment. Thus some aspects of illness and impairment are disabling. But disability has nothing to do with impairment.* (C. Thomas 1999: 39; emphasis original)

Her answer to this 'definitional riddle' is explained in terms of a 'residual equation of "disability" with "restrictions of activity" in some social modellist writings' (C. Thomas 1999: 39). That is to say, there have been two contrasting interpretations of disability in circulation. There is the 'relational' approach associated with the UPIAS formulation, where disability stems from the social barriers imposed on people with impairments, and there is the 'property' (or 'category') approach adopted in the ICIDH, where disability is defined as a property of individuals. Given the adherence of medical sociologists to an ICIDH framework, they have interpreted the social model as saying that all disability (that is, restrictions of activity) is socially caused (Bury 1996). It is fairly easy to demonstrate that this claim is false (Bickenbach 1993; French 1993). However, the relational approach does not locate all restrictions of activity in social barriers, and does not claim that impairment has no consequences for social participation. Instead, the analytical (and empirical) problem has been phrased in terms of identifying those circumstances in which it is impairment rather than disability that is more responsible.

For Thomas, 'impairment effects' (1999: 42–4) arise when the blind person cannot drive a car (safely) because of her impairment, or someone cannot play for her local basketball team because of a mobility impairment. However, from a relational perspective, such restrictions give rise to disability only if driving a car and running to work become conditions for obtaining paid employment.

Experiencing impairment and disability

The debates around impairment and disability have highlighted a clash between social model approaches and the dominant sociological approaches to 'chronic illness and disability' within medical sociology. They have denied that the social exclusion of people with impairments is due solely, or even predominantly, to the actions of a 'disabling society'. Social model accounts have been characterized as presenting an 'oversocialized' picture that downgrades individuals' experiences and meanings as well as wider social contexts (G. Williams 1996). Social model analyses are depicted as 'unidimensional' and 'reductionist' (Bury 1997: 138), and little more than an exercise in 'Marxist labelling' (p. 137).

Medical sociology, chronic illness and disability

For its part, the literature on medical sociology has been preoccupied with studying the experience of 'chronic illness and disability', but as defined from a 'property' approach in the ICIDH (Barnes and Mercer 1996a,b). Studies explored the meanings attributed to different conditions as negotiated across socio-cultural contexts. They shifted the analytical focus away from professional definitions and labels, and the 'mechanics of functional limitations and activity restriction'

(G. Williams 1998), to explore people's understanding of illness and impairment.

> Within rehabilitation, the environment has been defined for the most part as a physical phenomenon, a set of discrete obstacles or barriers, which add to and amplify the problems of impairment afflicting individuals. Within disability theory, the environment is regarded as the expression of power, a universe of discrimination and oppression within which disability is created. The sociological study of chronic illness and disability has tended to define the environment as something arising out of the symbolic and social interaction that takes place between individuals and their worlds as they negotiate their everyday lives. (G. Williams 1996: 195)

Mike Bury's outline of a 'socio-medical model of disabling illness' (1997: 116) distinguishes two types of meaning associated with having a chronic illness or 'disability' (that is, experiencing activity limitations): first, as *'consequence'*, which refers to its impact on the person's everyday roles and relationships; and second, as *'significance'*, which relates to the cultural meanings and symbolic significance surrounding specific conditions (p. 124).

The first examines how symptoms interfere with everyday routines, including close personal relationships, work and leisure activities. People may encounter difficulties in 'keeping up' with others or undertaking tasks that have hitherto been taken for granted (Anderson and Bury 1988). This has suggested different 'styles of adjustment' to chronic illness in terms of 'accommodation', 'active denial', 'secondary gain' and 'resignation' (Radley and Green 1987). However, such calculations are problematic in conditions such as arthritis and multiple sclerosis, where symptoms are unpredictable or not immediately visible.

Questions about the 'significance' of illness centre on how far, and in what ways, illness and impairment attract a different response across cultures and social groups? Susan Sontag (1991) illustrates in her studies of 'dread diseases' how conditions such as tuberculosis, cancer and HIV/AIDS have attracted particular symbolism in Western societies. Individuals must live as much with the fear and uncertainty attached to the condition as with its physical symptoms.

Further complexity arises where the 'felt' or anticipated stigma associated with a condition such as epilepsy is deemed 'worse' than the 'enacted' stigma or the actual experience of discrimination (Schneider and Conrad 1983; Scambler and Hopkins 1986).

If the general assumption is that the social meaning of impairment varies significantly, across social contexts, over time and across cultures, the specific research issue has been the impact of 'chronic illness and disability' on self-identity, and its consequences for everyday activities. An immediate answer is that different impairments have different trajectories. Indeed, researchers have argued that disabled people are not always as obsessed with seeking approval and avoiding embarrassing situations as interactionist studies have always suggested (Higgins 1981).

The dilemmas confronting individuals with a 'chronic illness and disability' are summarized as follows:

> First, is the *biographical disruption* brought about by such illness and the initial attempts to deal with the uncertainty it brings; second, there is the *impact of treatment* on everyday life, where this is relevant; and third, is the long-term *adaptation and management of illness* and disability which is undertaken as people respond and try to reconstruct normal life. (Bury 1997: 123)

The onset of such conditions carries a particular threat of 'biographical disruption' in a society that values an active, independent life-style. Individuals must construct a new self-identity in line with a more restricted, isolated and less autonomous way of life (Charmaz 1983).

For those who acquire their impairment, as opposed to being born with it, there are two main ways to mitigate biographical disruption (Bury 1997: 125–6): first, by constructing an account of what has happened and why, so that it is possible to repair, or in some way develop a 'narrative reconstruction' that reduces the threat posed to everyday routines and meanings (G. Williams 1984a); and second, by according the condition some 'legitimacy', in the sense that the chronic illness is acknowledged as a part of the individual's changed life-style. None the less, how a disabled person's self-identity is affected will depend in part on the nature of the impairment, their social and material circumstances, and the stage in the life cycle at which it occurs.

The impact of medical treatment is a further concern. Thus, the effects of surgical and radiation treatment may have a profound effect on a person's body image and social relationships. Michael Kelly (1996) explores this in the case of ileostomy patients. The changed body requires constant and delicate surveillance and regulation, often to keep things hidden from others. For others, body maintenance activities that were once routine and private, such as washing and going to the toilet, become major hurdles. Perhaps intimate tasks can now be accomplished only with help from others. This may lead to a reconceptualization of the individual's identity and self-image to incorporate loss of physical sensation, dependence on others, and exclusion from valued social activities.

Such concerns represent attempts to acquire some greater control over their lives and return to 'normality' (Bury 1997). The emphasis shifts to a more active process of personal adaptation. Coping mechanisms include the strategies people adopt in terms of preferred choices and the social, financial and emotional resources available. The 'performance' that is required of people living with chronic illness and disability involves planning, rehearsal and evaluation of actions, undertaken with other people in mind, as people strive to maintain a positive self-identity and highlight the 'capable self' rather than the 'disabled self' (Corbin and Strauss 1985).

This extends into more phenomenological analyses of the subjectivity of the impairment experience. Attention turns to the reconstitution of the individual self, and the negotiation and renegotiation of identity through talk (Charmaz 1987). In Murphy's (1987) account of his own progressive impairment leading to quadriplegia, he refers to his 'savaged' selfhood (p. 90) and his 'new, foreign and unwelcome identity' (p. 109). He recounts a slow evacuation of his body and being driven back to the final refuge, his brain. There is also clear evidence of the reluctance of people to be witness to his experience: 'Some admit that they cannot stand what has happened to me, so they stay away' (Murphy 1987: 124). However, what starts as a sociological analysis often loses sight of the structures that shape experience. Autobiographical accounts risk being 'sucked into a vortex of subjectivity' that is uncoupled from a view of chronic illness and disability as 'the product of the complex relationships between individuals, milieux and social structures' (G. Williams 1998: 242).

Difference and identity

Much of the justification for concentrating on the experience of impairment emulated feminist claims about distinctive 'ways of knowing': 'the exclusive prerogative of those who have experienced an oppression or a lifestyle to define its politics' (Stacey 1997: 62). While the claim to privileged insight as a disabled person has endured in much disability writing, it has been increasingly challenged by an emphasis on 'difference' and on multiple or 'fractured' identities. This progressed from arguments by disabled women that mainstream feminism had ignored their specific standpoint and experiences to similar claims against the dominance of disabled men in disabled people's organizations and politics. The process then unfolded further to identify multiple layers of social division among the disabled population. Space was created for experiential standpoints on the basis of interaction between disability, impairment and a host of other potential social identities (in a post-modern world).

Certainly, experience is important as a way of 'making sense, both symbolically and narratively; as a struggle over material conditions and over meaning' (Brah 1992: 141). However, it does not necessarily lead to a collective challenge to disability as a form of social oppression, and in so far as it is inherently fluid, it inhibits recognition of commonalities across struggles. Indeed, standpoint experience may simply generate 'individualisation and fragmentation, instead of analysis. Feminism(s) has an obligation to go beyond citing experience in order to make connections which may not be visible from the purely experiential level alone. This is an interpretative and synthesising process which connects experience to understanding' (Maynard 1994: 23–4).

An associated criticism of 'experiential' studies is that they too often ignore power relations and wider contextual factors:

> experience is represented as unmediated: spoken words are placed directly on a page with no account given of how and where they came from, the power relations involved, the publishing deals signed, the editing and selection processes. Or researchers take as self-evident the identities of those whose experience is being documented . . . Our experience is part of a social, historical, cultural, economic, political process. (Skeggs 1995: 15)

Nor is there any reason to presume that disabled people with 'common' attributes (impairment) will share the same experiences, let alone translate these into similar forms or meanings of social action. This raises questions about the range of experiential standpoints across the disabled population. Any presumption of a single disabled people's position attracts criticism that it is based on a false essentialism. It is further contested because it leads to a hierarchy of difference, where expression of contrary experiences is rejected as 'flawed' if not an instance of 'false consciousness' (Young 1990).

Nevertheless, the 'celebration of difference' is problematic for many disabled people, particularly those whose impairments are debilitating, painful or perhaps associated with premature death. It is not always easy to identify with assertions that 'We can celebrate, and take pride in, our physical and intellectual differences' (Morris 1991: 189); but confronting disability, individually and collectively, has enabled many disabled people to reject traditional expectations that they should retreat into feelings of shame or embrace exclusion as what impairment requires. It is also the source of considerable disbelief and unease among non-disabled people: 'Non-disabled people can generally accept that a wheel-chair user cannot enter a building because of steps. Non-disabled people are much more threatened and challenged by the notion that a wheel-chair user could be pleased and proud to be the person he or she is' (Swain and French 2000: 570).

The variation in felt and expressed experiences of impairment and disability among people with accredited impairments raises a number of conceptual and empirical issues, as well as concerns about the impact on attempts to build a disability culture and politics. Thus there is often unease when writers call for studies of the 'psycho-emotional dimensions of disablism': Who are we? Who might we be? How might we change our lives? What are the social restrictions within us (in addition to external disabling barriers)? (C. Thomas 1999: 46). A specific concern is that this approach easily descends into a discussion of 'internalized oppression', in which disabled people dwell on the pain and the fears, the negative self-images and the low expectations (Mason 1990: 27). Disabled people are then represented as taking on their societal designation as 'worthless, of lesser value, unattractive, hopeless, stressed or insecure' (C. Thomas 1999: 47). This may be at the cost of eliminating any sense of agency to resist disablism.

It is here that studies of experience merge with current social theory debates about the social construction of difference and identity formation. One argument has been that there should be recognition that difference has become the prime moving force behind disability culture and politics (Young 1997). Having been marginalized for so long, disabled people have sought to turn their distinctive and hitherto demeaned experiences into positive identities. However, there is a risk that such experiential approaches many produce new 'totalizing fictions' as newly established categories such as gender and disability give way to recognition of new groupings, often emerging out of simultaneous oppressions or other fluctuating differences (Somers 1994: 610).

This post-structuralist or post-modernist preoccupation with difference has shifted attention from a comparison of disabled and non-disabled people to studies of divisions within the disabled population. It is as necessary from a post-structuralist perspective to 'deconstruct' these new identities as much as the traditional ones. This approach provides an immediate contrast with the writings of feminists such as Jenny Morris (1991, 1993a) and Susan Wendell (1989, 1996). While both authors refer to the social construction of disability, neither dismisses the view that there is an underlying reality or experience that differentiates disabled and non-disabled people because of necessarily different experiences of impairment and disability. Thus Wendell distances herself from literature that will 'deny or ignore bodily experience in favour of a fascination with bodily representations' (1996: 44), and talks about her 'emerging understanding of disability as socially constructed from biological differences between the disabled and non-disabled' (1996: 5). Morris is equally sensitive to difference, but tends to 'talk for' disabled women as if they are a unitary category (C. Thomas 1999: 108), in much the same way as disabled men have been criticized for speaking on behalf of all disabled people. This produces a basic divide in her writing between the 'impaired (not normal) body and the unimpaired (normal) body which exists prior to social differences' (C. Thomas 1999: 110).

According to Margaret Somers, one way to avoid turning a category such as gender or disability into a rigid framework for identity is to introduce the 'categorically destabilizing dimensions of *time, space,* and *relationality*' (Somers 1994: 606). She recommends adoption of a narrative approach that moves from the study of observable behaviour (measured in terms of values and norms, interests and preferences) to examine how people use stories to make sense of their everyday experiences and emotions. The promise of this approach is that it allows us to analyse the ways in which identity is socially produced, and thus varies historically and across cultures, while also integrating the notion of the individual as an active agent. From this perspective, the disabled people's movement offers one instance of a 'counter-narrative' that has enabled many people with impairments to 'make sense' of their lives in novel and constructive ways. The designation of an individual as a 'disabled' person does not result in a fixed identity, but should be thought of as a narrative that is constantly being reworked or 'retold' (Somers 1994; C. Thomas 1999).

While there are problems with an essentialist starting point, this does not let post-structuralism off the hook. There is an immediate contradiction in the insistence on deconstruction as an analytical approach. But, equally important, it runs counter to any explanation that starts from 'materialist' or 'realist' premises but claims (at least) to avoid charges of biological reductionism. While deconstructionist arguments presume that all other approaches are reductionist, we reject this, and look towards innovative analyses that are more eclectic in bringing together studies of disabled people's lived experiences, social constructionism and materialism.

Disabled minds and bodies

With the arrival of post-structuralism, sociological studies turned to consider the social production of medical knowledge, and more specifically of the body (Turner 1984, 1992; Shilling 1993; Williams and Bendelow 1998). Whereas disability theorists were content to leave definitions of the body and impairment to medicine, or explored a diluted embodied experience, post-structuralist writers embarked on a deconstruction of claims that impairment and disability occupied separate worlds. Instead of accepting the scientific claim that the body is 'natural' or 'pre-social', it was granted, like disability, its own history:

> Not only has it been perceived, interpreted, and represented differently in different epochs, but it has also been lived differently, brought into being within widely dissimilar material cultures, subjected to various technologies and means of control, and incorporated into different rhythms of production and consumption, pleasure and pain. (Gallagher and Laqueur 1987: p. vii)

Post-structuralism privileges the cultural level by dismissing notions of a pre-social body and locating it instead as a discursive product of power/knowledge (S. Williams 2000). Following this path, Donna Haraway argued that 'Neither our personal bodies nor our social bodies may be seen as natural in the sense of existing outside the self-creating process of human labour' (Haraway 1990: 10). More specifically, the significance of post-structuralist approaches lies 'first in deconstructing all and every identity, and second in laying bare the ways in which the body itself is constructed and maintained as disabled' (Shildrick and Price 1996: 96).

This represented a 'seismic shift' in conceptualizing the body compared with the mainstream of both sociology and disability studies (Paterson and Hughes 1999b: 30). 'Both treat it as a pre-social, inert, physical object, as discrete, palpable and separate from the self' (Hughes and Paterson 1997: 329), even though disability struggles have clearly been embodied in confronting the medicalization and infantilization of disability (Paterson and Hughes 1999b: 32).

Thus, Bill Hughes and Kevin Paterson (1997) take the early social model writers to task for following the 'Cartesian divide' in Western thinking and simply assimilating the medical discourse, rather than developing a non-reductionist social theory of impairment. 'In this context there is no dualistic outside/in or inside/out models of emancipation. Politics today, is as much about aesthetics (formed and forming bodies) as it is about economic and public life' (Paterson and Hughes 1999a: 600).

It was during the 1980s that the social construction of the disabled body-mind gathered momentum. Fixed or universal signifiers of bodies, minds and identity are rejected. In contrast, bodies are made 'real' (and 'normalized') through a set of discursive practices, just as feminists had argued in the case of supposedly irreducible and unchanging notions of gender and sexuality (Fawcett 2000). The spotlight was turned on the production and organization of biological difference (and impairment) through power/knowledge relations (Foucault 1980). Needless to say 'To both the biomedical profession with its fantasy of descriptive objectivity, and to the (disability rights movement) with its investment in the notion that impairment can be separated off from disability, the claim is anathema' (Price and Shildrick 1998: 234).

The same criticism is directed at disabled self-help groups who establish their own alternative 'normality' or essence as the basis for group identification and cohesion (Shildrick and Price 1996). The boundaries of sameness and difference are constantly changing. Even though writers on disability have always stressed the importance of language and terminology, social model accounts always discounted the power of discursive practices (except as ideologies), and failed 'to conceptualize a mutually constitutive relationship between impairment and disability which is both materially and discursively (socially) produced' (Corker and French 1999: 6). Hence the significance of deconstructing discourses on the body, as forms of regulation, but also as a way of changing or 're-authoring' disabled people's lives. Mairian Corker (1998a, 1998b, 1999) vividly illustrates the potential of this deconstructionist strategy in her studies of interactions between Deaf people, deaf people and the disabled people's movement. She argues against the essentialism of both Deaf activists and social model writers as they seek a discourse that marginalizes new 'Others'.

However, deconstructionist analyses fail to address issues regarding the production and maintenance of discourses as well as their demise. It is a disappointment to find that the 'transgressive resistance' of post-structuralism can be demonstrated by nothing more startling than, for example, 'the visually impaired woman who greets you in the evening on the street but cannot see you in the light of day' (Shildrick and Price 1996: 107).

Rehabilitation discourses

The growing importance attached to medical rehabilitation for disabled people offers a valuable case study of an emerging discourse. It takes as its starting point the potential for reconstitution of the body and self after acquiring an impairment. While rehabilitation remains within a broad personal tragedy approach, it breaks new ground in laying emphasis on the possibilities for a 'second chance' (Giddens 1991).

Wendy Seymour explores these issues in *Remaking the Body* (1998), which is a study of a group of people who had recently acquired a spinal chord injury and the ways in which a particular discourse was employed to get them to address their 'damaged' bodies and the associated uncertainties and fears about their future prospects. Seymour highlights their sense of frailty, vulnerability, pain and dependence. This focus is heightened by late twentieth-century Western culture's targeting of the body as a primary arena for 'mediating the tensions and insecurities of modern life' (Seymour 1998: 19). Health professionals encouraged their patients to map out new choices and possible changes in their lives not contemplated prior to the acquisition of their impairment.

It is very apparent that rehabilitation discourse is invested with a moral notion of what bodies should be like. It is often biased towards male values and life-styles (Morris 1989). There is a determination to fit the disabled person back into society, and thereby achieve 'a good result' (Seymour 1998: 21). One route is the use of technology, because it offers better functional performance, perhaps some repair or more sensation. Yet professional discourse also concentrated on the merits of regaining some 'normal' functions, such as the capacity to walk. It tends to categorize individuals with a mobility impairment or injury – for example, as 'confined' to a wheelchair – whereas several studies that have looked at lay experiences have demonstrated that the potential for mobility offered by the wheelchair is evaluated much more positively, certainly over what are seen as the dubious attractions of limited mobility using crutches (Tremblay 1996).

It may be some distance from rehabilitation discourse, but there are parallels encouraged by science fiction's fascination with reconstituted – part human and part machine – bodies. The potential of science and technology to create new bodies or regenerate lost physical and intellectual capabilities has given rise to extravagant flights of academic fantasy. According to Donna Haraway, some disabled people epitomize cyborgs or transhuman subjects: 'The cyborg is a kind of dis-assembled and reassembled, post-modern collective and personal self' (Haraway 1991: 163).

Certainly, biomedical technology, alongside cosmetic surgery and the fitness and beauty industries, help reconstruct bodies (Williams and Bendelow 1998). Yet the technological fix outlined in some cyborg accounts presumes a capacity to overturn impairment (and disability) that few disabled people will recognize or necessarily applaud. Haraway delights in the 'perverse' aspect of technology that enables (some) disabled people to turn the tables on 'normal' human beings, although her 'half a human being' status simply diminishes the wheelchair user, the person with a prosthesis, or the individual who uses a hearing aid.

Nevertheless, changing medical treatment and intervention mean that profound ethical dilemmas have multiplied around the body, its status and meaning. Claims abound that the disabled body can be saved by 'magic bullet' medical interventions, despite disabled people's mixed feelings.

Embodiment and body projects

From a post-modern perspective, the fixed, biological body has looked more and more uncertain in recent years – with a focus on body projects and technological and allied interventions. The images projected by consumer culture are infused with notions of youth, health and physical beauty (Featherstone 1991). Hence individual experiences and identity are importantly shaped by social judgements about the 'normal', 'attractive' and 'fit' body.

Recent theorizations of the body in Western societies have stressed how a combination of life-style and identity social movements along with social changes ranging from developments in medical technology to moves towards a consumer society have rendered the body as an 'icon of contemporary consumerism' (Seymour 1998: p. v). The cultivation of body image has become a principal mechanism for the presentation of self and 'being in control' in late modern society. Corporeal criteria have become central to representing personal qualities and moral capacities (Crawford 1980). Contemporary concern over anorexia nervosa and bulimia vividly illustrate the importance of cultural ideals of beauty, body shape and appearance.

The concern has moved from fitting bodies for factory production to pursuing the demands of the consumer society. 'Burgeoning new industries have developed sophisticated pharmaceutical, surgical, mechanical and computerised means to extend the potential of our frail, unreliable, inefficient and vulnerable bodies' (Seymour 1998: 6). Bodies have increasingly come to signify attitude, control and vitality (Giddens 1990). The emphasis is on the maintenance and marketing of attractive bodies:

> [W]ith the decline of religious frameworks which constructed and sustained existential and ontological certainties residing outside the individual, and the massive rise of the body in consumer culture as a bearer of symbolic value, there is a tendency for people in high modernity to place ever more

importance on the body as constitutive of self. (Shilling 1993: 3)

The 'body is becoming increasingly a phenomenon of options and choices' (Shilling 1993: 3), but this raises new possibilities and dilemmas. The less it approximates idealized images, the lower its 'exchange value' (Featherstone 1991: 177). 'Body work is the principal activity of everyday life, and as embodied actors, we actively employ our bodies to create or alter the experience of being a body within the social world. Having and being a body lie at the core of all self-creation and world-building activities' (Seymour 1998: 177). In addition, physical capital has become increasingly important in contributing to cultural capital – with the pursuit of beauty and fitness – in what is becoming an increasingly 'somatic society' (Turner 1992). These disciplinary regimes rebound on the disabled body, however, and on those disabled people who have fewer resources with which to implement their own preferences whether of 'maintenance' or 'improvement'.

This leads to a central criticism of discourse analysis: that the material body 'disappears' in the sense that little attention is given to people's experiences of either their sick bodies or of disability. The primary emphasis is on the body as an object of power/knowledge rather than a lived entity. It was not until his later writings that Foucault acknowledged forms of subjectivity that recognized the possibilities for 'resistance' and 'overcoming'.

We see most theoretical and political potential in exploring the experience of embodiment in ways that represent the body as both a 'biological phenomenon' and a 'social production' (Seymour 1998: 12). Indeed, it is this focus on individual experience of impairment and disability that provides a path to understanding agency and identity (Hughes and Paterson 1997). The potential to mould the body, whether one with an impairment or not, is in keeping with a sense of self that is located 'in the capacity to keep a narrative going', although this is always at risk because of the contingent and changing character of (self) knowledge (Giddens 1991: 53–4). Moreover, the claim that social oppression is embodied encourages the conflation of private troubles and public issues (Paterson and Hughes 1999b). It also points to possibilities for reconstruction and for revaluing the body and impairment.

Hence the significance of an eclectic approach that incorporates the subjective experiences or phenomenology of embodiment as well as the power of social discourse in the construction of bodies, while recognizing the broader context within which the body can be known and understood (Turner 1992; Shilling 1993). From a phenomenological perspective, interpretations of sickness, pain and impairment illuminate an attack on the embodied self. In addition, Foucault's influence has led to portraying disabled people as largely passive witnesses to discursive practices. This needs to be replaced by a wider appreciation of ways of understanding embodiment. This also underpins Carol Thomas's argument for an incorporation of 'impairment effects' within a feminist materialist 'non-reductionist ontology of the body' (1999: 143). The aim is to put 'minds back into bodies, bodies back into society and society back into the body' (Williams and Bendelow 1998: 3).

Review

In this chapter we have examined the criticism of social model approaches to disability that the exclusion of impairment weakens the understanding of both impairment and disability and entails a restricted disability politics. It has been argued that there is considerable confusion over the explanation of 'impairment effects', primarily because the competing accounts use contrasting approaches to disability: one categorical, the other relational. It is our view that the relational approach does and should underpin a social analysis of disability. Moreover, it focuses on the impact of exclusionary social barriers on people with impairments, rather than attempting a social explanation of all functional restrictions.

The disability literature on impairment has also been divided between competing accounts of a social-constructionist approach. The embrace of post-structuralist versions now exerts a considerable influence on disability studies, but as the discussion of difference and identity illustrates, a more nuanced approach is necessary that presumes a consciousness of self that is developed and sustained in the interaction between a 'real' body and a 'real' social environment. There is a considerable literature within medical sociology exploring experiences of living with a 'chronic illness and disability' on which to draw, but it lacks the sense of the individual/body as a creative force. The body is a site for reframing one's self-identity, and bodies are more sculpted and engineered than ever before. We also accept that bodies and minds are more than an artefact of discourse. This provides an entry point for disability analyses that explore the relationship between an active, material body and the lived experience of embodiment.

5
Culture, Media and Representation

In previous chapters, we have concentrated on analyses of social oppression that explore those dimensions related to the social division of labour – marginalization, powerlessness and exploitation. These refer to structural and institutional relations that restrict opportunities for material resources and life chances. We now turn to consider cultural domination, or 'cultural imperialism' (Young 1990). This denotes a form of social oppression in which groups experience symbolic devaluation, in the ways that set them apart as 'Other', submerged in negative stereotypes. Most often, culturally oppressed groups such as disabled people also experience material disadvantages and relative powerlessness. By contrast, non-disabled people's greater access to the means of communication and representation effectively ensures the dominance of the world-view and values of able-bodied 'normality'.

This chapter has three main objectives: first, to review key contributions to the analysis of culture and its relationship to society, the economy and politics; second, to outline the representation of disability in mainstream culture, including debates around 'audience effects' of these media; and finally, to examine the development of a disability culture, including disability arts, that seeks to offer a positive alternative to negative stereotypes and the hegemony of 'able-bodiedism', while allowing for 'difference' among disabled people.

Analysing culture

Sociological studies of culture have adopted a broad interpretation to include symbolic aspects of human society, such
as beliefs, rituals, customs, values and norms, as well as work
patterns, leisure activities and material goods. Whereas values
are 'abstract ideals', norms encompass socially acceptable
rules or guidelines. These guidelines describe a diffuse view
of culture as a shared 'way of life' – what we think, how we
act, and the material and symbolic objects with which we
identify.

To function as a member of a society, it is important to
learn its cultural rules and assumptions, including what (or
who) is considered 'normal' and acceptable. Culture is a link
with the past as well as a guide to the present. It includes the
ties that bind as well as what divide human groups. And as
cultures demonstrate continuity, so too they exhibit a degree
of flux and capacity for creativity.

The definition of culture has shifted from a location in the
artistic and intellectual ideas and activities of an elite to incorporate the pursuits of the whole population. T. S. Eliot's
evocation of mid-twentieth-century English culture included
a multi-class celebration: 'Derby Day, Henley Regatta,
Cowes, the twelfth of August, a cup final, the dog races, the
pin table, the dart board, Wensleydale cheese, boiled cabbage
cut into sections, beetroot in vinegar, nineteenth-century
Gothic churches, and the music of Elgar' (Eliot 1968: 104).

Any attempt to produce a similar list at the beginning of
the twenty-first century will probably come up with very
different things, or perhaps find that the tremendous emphasis on diversity and difference makes compilation of a
common list almost impossible. The significance of these
changes in the form and content of national cultures feeds
into wider debates about the relationship between culture
and society, particularly its material base, and the role
played by culture (and more specifically the mass media) in
social control and social change. In the mid-twentieth century, there were two very different interpretations. Marxists
and Critical Theorists argued that modern (mass) culture was
orchestrated by the dominant classes to promote passivity in

the subordinate population, while more pluralistic accounts regarded the media as subject to market competition and consumer choice and only one among many competing sources of political influence in a liberal democratic society (Kellner 1989).

By the 1960s and 1970s, studies of culture had divided again, between refurbished neo-Marxist analyses and new structuralist analyses that stressed the importance of language and the 'scientific' decoding of texts and signs (Hall 1997). Our interest lies with neo-Marxist analyses of the cultural domain as an arena of political struggle. A key stimulus was Antonio Gramsci's analysis of 'hegemony', and how the willing consent of subordinate groups might be achieved through the dominant group's direction of the production and consumption of cultural activities (see chapter 2). This approach was developed by Stuart Hall and his colleagues (e.g. Hall and Jefferson 1976; Hall 1980) in their analyses of 'subcultures' (spanning 'race', gender, sexuality and youth), as potential sources for counter-hegemonies or resistance. The emphasis shifted towards multiple, hybrid cultures characterized by fluid and contested boundaries (Kuper 1999: 216), while cultural politics changed 'from a struggle over the relations of representation to a politics of representation itself' (Hall 1988). In the case of disability, studies began to explore how hegemonic views are secured and challenged, including debates over identity and what it means to be a disabled person or part of a disabled culture.

More recently, studies of culture have come under the influence of post-structuralism and post-modernism (Inglis 1993). Following Michel Foucault, the emphasis on power/knowledge has concentrated on cultural production through discourse. In place of ideological domination, Foucault inserts linguistic-discursive practices. Historically, medical discourse has been pre-eminent in redrawing the boundaries between 'able-bodied normality' and the 'disabled other' (Hughes and Paterson 1997). Post-structuralist analyses 'deconstruct' dominant and 'hidden' readings and representations, and attempt to 'give voice' to those who have been marginalized or silenced.

Cultural representations of disability

Historically, across European cultures, there has been a 'fascination with spectacles of difference' (Mitchell and Snyder 2001: 210), with a concentration on 'defective' or 'abnormal' bodies and minds. The 'otherness' of disabled people has been exploited as a source of 'entertainment' as well as to stir the fears and emotions of the non-disabled population. In ancient Greece and Rome, 'it would almost seem as if no fashionable household was complete without a generous sprinkling of dwarfs, mutes, cretins, eunuchs and hunchbacks, whose principle duty appears to have been to undergo degrading and painful humiliation in order to provide amusement at dinner parties and other festive occasions' (Garland 1995: 46).

The public display of perceived bodily abnormalities continued throughout the Middle Ages. Many royal courts in Europe retained people of short stature as 'court jesters' or kept a complement of 'fools' – including people with cognitive impairments and learning difficulties, as well as others who feigned 'idiocy' to provide amusement. It was also common practice for people with perceived 'deformities' to be put on display at village fairs, while some peasant parents 'toured the countryside displaying for money recently born infants with birth defects' (Gerber 1996: 43). The public exhibition of the inmates of 'mad-houses' and institutions continued this practice into the seventeenth and eighteenth centuries.

By the nineteenth century, such displays had developed into 'freak shows', which offered a 'formally organized exhibition of people with alleged physical, mental or behavioural difference at circuses, fairs, carnivals or other amusement venues' (Bogdan 1996: 25). These flourished in Europe and North America in the nineteenth and early part of the twentieth century, and were complemented by the so-called 'Ugly Laws' in the USA which placed social restrictions on those whose physical appearance might offend or frighten 'normal' people (Bogdan 1996; Gerber 1996). These prohibited the appearance of individuals who were 'diseased, maimed, mutilated, or in any way deformed so as to be an unsightly, or disgusting object' (Centre for Independent Living 1982: 249).

Disabled people and their organizations took the lead in challenging this tyranny of 'able-bodied' assumptions in mainstream culture. As Paul Hunt argued, disabled people 'are set apart from the ordinary' as if a direct 'challenge' to commonly held societal values. This attitude characterizes disability in industrial capitalist societies as a 'personal tragedy' in which 'people's shocked reaction to the "obvious deviant" stimulates their own deepest fears and difficulties, their failure to accept themselves as they really are and the other person simply as "other" ' (Hunt 1966a: 152).

Others have regarded the cultural meanings associated with 'dread diseases', such as cancer and HIV/AIDS, as so powerful that 'it is hardly possible to take up one's residence in the kingdom of the ill unprejudiced by the lurid metaphors with which it has been landscaped' (Sontag 1991: 3). Moreover, corporeal descriptors (such as 'cancer', 'insane', 'crippled') are widely employed as shorthand for social, political and economic crises and calamities. And yet, while illness and impairment most often trigger negative reactions, they have also been associated with a partial romanticization. For example, in the nineteenth century, tuberculosis, or 'consumption', became closely linked with individual creativity and artistic sensitivity, as in the case of well-known novelists and poets, including Robert Louis Stevenson, Katherine Mansfield and John Keats (Sontag 1991).

Most typically, then, Western cultures identify and mark out certain people as 'different' or 'Other' – particularly those perceived as having flawed or ugly bodies.

> Our disability frightens people. They don't want to think that this is something which could happen to them. So we become separated from our common humanity, treated as fundamentally different and alien. Having put up clear barriers between us and them, non-disabled people further hide their fear and discomfort by turning us into objects of pity, comforting themselves by their own kindness and generosity. (Morris 1991: 192)

Louis Battye (1966) offers an early analysis of the literary representation of impairment as impotence in D. H.

Lawrence's *Lady Chatterley's Lover*. Children's stories are replete with their own brand of courage, fear, pity and abhorrence (Shearer 1981). Disability writers note that disabled people are absent in culture, but their primary grievance is that, when present, they are represented in a wholly stereotypical way. The concentration on stereotypes such as Shakespeare's Richard III, Dickens's Tiny Tim and Melville's Captain Ahab have been supplemented by wide-ranging and in-depth studies of the medicalization of disability, with its curative and rehabilitative themes, as well as its enduring association with the 'grotesque' and supernatural (Snyder and Mitchell 2001). 'What we fear, we often stigmatize and shun and sometimes seek to destroy. Popular entertainments depicting disabled characters allude to these fears and prejudices or address them obliquely or fragmentarily, seeking to reassure us about ourselves' (Longmore 1987: 66). Further, 'The most prevalent image in films and especially in television during the past several decades has been the maladjusted disabled person' (p. 70).

Academic studies of impairment and disability representation took off slowly through the late 1980s, particularly in the USA (Biklen and Bogdan 1977; Zola 1985; Gartner and Joe 1987; Klobas 1988). These point overwhelmingly to the negative cultural stereotyping of people with impairments. The 'metaphorical uses of disability are well documented' (Zola 1985: 5). The primary themes of pity and fear are supplemented by diverse images of menace, loathing, innocence and courage. Disabled people are depicted 'in the passive voice' and as 'victims' or 'sufferers'. These images permeate media aimed specifically at children (Quicke 1985; Davidson et al. 1994). Popular cartoon characters, such as Elmer Fudd and Mr Magoo, are set apart because of their physical and intellectual 'defects'.

In one of the most cited collections, *Images of the Disabled, Disabling Images* (Gartner and Joe 1987), Laurence Kriegel concludes, after reviewing sources as diverse as *Lady Chatterley's Lover* and *Moby Dick*, that 'The world of the crippled and disabled is strange and dark, and it is held up to judgment by those who live in fear of it. The cripple is the creature who has been deprived of his ability to create a self. . . . He must accept definition from outside the boundaries of his own existence' (Kriegel 1987: 33).

TV portrayals of impairment and disability are the most widely researched. The absence of disabled people, and their lack of appearance in major roles, are long-established findings in American studies (Zola 1985). People with impairments lead one-dimensional lives, as dependent, unproductive and in need of care. The dramatic focus centres on their interaction with health care or social welfare professionals. As Harlan Hahn (1989) notes, the 'good parts' of ordinary lives – love, romance and sex – are largely absent or not stressed in disabled character's lives. Nor is there much interest in exploring disabling social barriers. Instead, impairment is portrayed as something to be eliminated or overcome (Longmore 1997).

Content analyses of the British media provide a similar picture. For example, Guy Cumberbatch and Ralph Negrine (1992) monitored television output over a six-week period during 1988. Their central findings, reinforced by more recent studies (Ross 1997), are that television programmes consistently adhere to a 'personal tragedy' approach. The most prevalent story-lines link disabled people with medical treatment or cure, together with programmes focusing on their 'special achievements'. Moreover, the representations of disabled people are highly stereotypical, depicting them not as ordinary members of society, but using them to evoke emotions of pity, fear or admiration. Newspaper reporting of disability has attracted similar criticism (Smith and Jordan 1991). A limited number of themes dominate newspaper coverage, mainly health, fund-raising, charity, and personal tragedy stories.

John Berger's *Ways of Seeing* (1972) details the social positioning of bodies through their visual representation. Photography was notoriously at the centre of scientific initiatives to classify physiognomy and impairment, as well as central to the Nazi promotion of the classical 'Aryan' body. However, attempts at more positive images too easily slip into 'denial, disavowal or suppression of the struggle and oppression' (Hevey 1992: 103). This is demonstrated in media coverage of President F. D. Roosevelt whereby only a handful of photographs out of 35,000 showed him as a wheelchair user (p. 102).

A summary audit of media's preference for 'crippling images' includes a fondness for 'wonder cure' stories, the role of charity appeals, the invisibility of disabled people on television, the stereotyped portrayal of disabled characters, and the under-employment of disabled people in TV and radio (Karpf 1988). The most frequently documented cultural stereotypes represent the disabled person as pitiable and pathetic, an object of violence, as sinister and evil, as atmosphere or curio, as 'super-cripple', as an object of ridicule, as their own worst enemy, as burden, as sexually abnormal, as incapable of participating fully in community life, and as 'normal' (Barnes 1992). While the latter suggests a solitary positive viewpoint, it is also the least widely expressed, and its representation of 'normality' largely ignores the social oppression of disabled people.

More recently, this focus on the under- or mis-representation of disabled people has given way to studies highlighting the mediation of other social factors, such as gender, ethnicity, class and age. Studies of disabled women in literature suggest that they are used primarily as a metaphor for addressing some broader theme. Thus, dramatic interest focuses on their role as tragic or saintly figures, who may perhaps be 'saved' by an 'able-bodied' man:

> In all these instances, disability sets the tone for the women's interaction with others. Her competence at homemaking chores, her educational attainments, or her personality have little effect upon the attitudes of others toward her. As other characters react to her disability they are not concerned about her competence, but something much deeper and harder to define. Disability seems to undermine the very roots of her womanhood. (Kent 1987: 63).

Fine and Asch (1988) argue that disabled women are alternatively portrayed as sexually promiscuous or asexual/innocents, denied opportunities to express their sexuality in everyday ways such as clothes, hair style or intimate sexual activity. The reluctance to depict disabled women as sexual beings, or in traditional female roles as wives and mothers, is explored by Helen Meekosha and Leanne Dowse (1997). They illustrate the contradiction between the support by the disabled people's movement for images of disabled people in 'normal' roles and the desire of feminists to challenge gender stereotypes. Equally, the polarization of 'normal' masculinity and disabled impotency accentuates the image of disability as a personal tragedy.

This has led to a growing interest in the cultural representation of the 'normal' body or what Lennard Davis terms the 'hegemony of normalcy': 'One can find in almost any novel . . . a kind of surveying of the terrain of the body, an attention to difference – physical, mental and national' (Davis 1995: 41). These themes are pursued in Rosemarie Garland Thomson's (1997) analysis of disability representation in American culture, which spans the traditional freak show, sentimental novels such as *Uncle Tom's Cabin*, and contemporary African-American fiction. She claims that the 'cultural intolerance of anomaly is one of the most pervasive themes in Western thought' (Thomson 1997: 33). Her study draws heavily on contemporary literary, feminist and social theory, particularly post-modernism, to examine how 'corporeal deviance' is a 'product of cultural rules' about 'able-bodiedness': 'Constructed as the embodiment of corporeal insufficiency and deviance, the physically disabled body becomes a repository for social anxieties about such troubling concerns as vulnerability, control and identity' (Thomson 1997: 6). Most importantly, Thomson also explores an emerging counter-representation: for example, in the novels of Toni Morrison, 'physically disabled or anomalous black women triumph', and the novels 'repudiate stigmatization itself' (Thomson 1997).

Stereotypical and distorted representations of people with physical impairments have been standard fare in cinema film. In the most comprehensive history of such disability representation, Martin Norden concludes that 'the history of physical disability images in the movies has mostly been a history of distortion in the name of maintaining an ableist society' (Norden 1994: 314).

As a visual medium, cinema uses pictures to reveal character, so the physical and emotional 'cripple' was a regular amalgam. The cinema also inherited the entrepreneurial traditions of the freak show, or, as Cecil B. De Mille remarked: 'affliction is much more saleable' (quoted in Norden 1994: 71). While a range of negative stereotypes has predominated, there have been some positive changes in this imagery. Norden identifies an early exploitative phase (1890s–1930s), when highly stylized images of 'comic stick-figures, freakish beasts, or pitiable objects' (p. 314) predominated. This was followed by a more exploratory phase (1930s–1970s) in which individuals struggled to overcome their personal tragedy. Moreover, up to the 1930s, clear gender stereotypes prevailed – typically 'Sweet Innocent' females, as opposed to male 'Comic Misadventurers', 'Tragic Victims', 'Noble Warriors' and 'Obsessive Avengers' (Norden 1994: 315). He distinguishes a third phase (1970s–1990s) when impairment was dealt with in a more 'incidental' way across very different contexts: rehabilitation, struggles for social justice, and personal relationships, including sexuality. Nevertheless, outright condemnation of film movies for disseminating 'nightmarish images of disability as a threat to social stability' (Snyder and Mitchell 2001: 369) must be set against individual exceptions such as the easy integration of a Deaf character in *Four Weddings and a Funeral*.

Paul Darke explores similar themes in his textual analysis of disability in films such as *The Elephant Man* (Darke 1994) and *When Billy Broke his Head and Other Tales of Wonder* (Darke 1995). He categorizes the latter as a *rite de passage* movie, in which Billy Golfus, newly impaired after a motorcycle accident, explores the meaning of disabled masculinity in American society. Darke (1998) further explores what he terms 'normality drama'. This is a genre that uses abnormal/impaired characters to represent a perceived threat to dominant views, thus indirectly rationalizing their social marginalization.

One of the most widely cited attempts to locate an aesthetic and theoretical analysis of bodily representation within a broader concern with social and political context is advanced by David Hevey in his study of charity advertising, *The Creatures Time Forgot* (1992). He examines how British charities 'market' particular impairments in ways parallel to the 'branding' of commercial products in their search for public support. A hallmark of the early charity approach is the stark image of the person with an impairment, usually in black and white, which centres on their physical 'flaw'. Its purpose is to evoke fear and sympathy in the viewer. 'Charity advertising sells fear, while commercial advertising sells desire' (Hevey 1992: 35). It sets up a 'dependent impairment, active charity dynamic' (pp. 35–6), and is no less than the 'visual flagship for the myth of the tragedy of impairment' (pp. 51–2) and a means of victim blaming. Charity representations accentuate pity for people with impairments and their general dependence and helplessness.

The aim is to stimulate an emotional reaction from the viewer that turns the subject into an object of desire/fear. This has particularly threatening consequences for many disabled women.

> There are also dangers here of the advertising industry moving from selling the beautiful and sculptured non-disabled body to selling the beautiful and sculptured disabled body. For women with degenerative or acquired disabilities, or illnesses not amenable to physical body sculpting, these images can further demoralize and undermine their sense of self-worth. (Meekosha and Dowse 1997: 97–8)

Nevertheless, some charities have attempted to move away from their reliance on disabling imagery. This approach has been categorized as, 'look at the ability not the disability'. Recent initiatives in Britain by SCOPE (formerly known as the Spastics Society) focused on prejudice and discrimination without dispensing entirely with a personal tragedy approach. The Leonard Cheshire Foundation followed suit in its 'Enabled' advertising campaign. Mencap, a charity for people with learning difficulties, replaced its tearful 'Little Stephen' logo with a more positive representation that embraced citizenship and social rights (Corbett and Ralph 1994: 11).

Overall, through the last quarter of the twentieth century, there has been a discernible rise in more 'positive' cultural and media images of disabled people. Since the 1980s, disabled characters have begun to appear in high-profile advertisements for Kodak films, Levi jeans and McDonalds (Longmore 1987). There are also more 'disabled' characters, although not all are played by actors with impairments, and disability story-lines are underplayed in British and American soaps and dramas (Pointon 1997).

Audiences and media effects

In analysing the media, attention is focused on the processes of encoding and decoding. Analysis of the production of these texts – their encoding – examines the social context and constraints in producing TV news items, newspaper stories and information on the internet. Why are specific stories selected as 'newsworthy' – including why some impairment groups rarely appear? How are these related to the technical constraints and demands on presenting items within different media?

The next, crucial question is about the decoding process: how do audiences receive and understand media information and messages? The literature divides between an answer which presumes both intent and desired impact, perhaps linked with a hidden agenda serving dominant interests, and another that suggests a more variable impact. This reinforces a further divide, between studies that posit a 'top-down' manipulation and those that allow for an uncertain audience response.

As the media have grown in importance through the twentieth century as mechanisms for communicating ideas and information, so their significance as a terrain of cultural politics has increased. There has been a widespread presumption, in both the American and the British literature on disability, that cultural and media imagery has a potent, if not direct, effect on its audience. This remains an empirical question, but it sits uneasily with recent characterizations of late twentieth-century culture that stress the significance of social and cultural diversity rather than homogeneity. This raises doubts about the capacity of the media to disseminate specific messages.

Hitherto, a straightforward 'hypodermic syringe' model has prevailed, in which the 'naturalness' of disability is promoted/reinforced across the range of cultural forms. Against this, a 'uses and gratifications' approach claimed that people are not simply inert or passive, but actively interpret media materials in accordance with their own needs and interests (McQuail 1972). Hence, assumptions that the media are always able to 'manufacture consent' to the dominant order

are set aside, by acknowledging that the media may be 'read'
in contrary ways, so that audiences sometimes revise or reject
intended messages (Hall 1980, 1997).

> Models tend to be static and do not necessarily reflect con-
> tradictory representations and change over time. They help us
> 'fit' media stories into boxes, but do not necessarily aid in a
> more complex analysis of the processes involved in disability
> construction. Thus overall, the variety of elements of media
> analysis necessary to understand disability cannot be reduced
> to a simple categorization of content, but require a complex
> sensitivity to multiple dimensions of the process. (Meekosha
> and Dowse 1997: 95)

The possibility of an active audience remains under-explored
in studies of the media and disability. Certainly, media
audiences will have already established views regarding
disability. Nevertheless, the media's pivotal role in the disse-
mination of information, images and opinions has been identified in HIV/AIDS (Kitzinger 1993) and in mental illness
(Philo 1996). Hence the widespread assumption that the
media's negative stereotypes of disabled people reinforce
existing patterns of discrimination, and in some instances, as
with highly stigmatized groups such as those with 'mental
illness', may contribute to a 'moral panic' about their
inclination to commit random acts of personal violence.

If it is accepted that audiences may interpret media information and representations in many different ways, it must
also be allowed that different audience 'readings' may in part
be attributed to confusion over whether the 'author' or those
involved more generally in cultural production always have
a 'message' that they are trying to get across. What 'reading'
should one place on H. G. Wells's short story 'The Country
of the Blind' published in 1904, which tells of a man called
Nunez who falls off a mountain into an isolated valley
populated entirely by people with congenital blindness. He
presumes wrongly, as it turns out, that 'in the Country of the
Blind, the One-eyed Man is King' (Wells 1979: 129). Issues
of 'able-bodied' superiority and the civilizing mission of the
non-disabled person abound, but in the end, the blind population reject Nunez (who represents 'civilization') in favour
of the 'obvious' merits of their own way of life. Again, film

representations often generate polarized interpretations among both academic and lay audiences (Shakespeare 1999). Is Tod Browning's 1932 classic horror film *Freaks* a break-through in disability representation or a 'misplaced' attempt to 'humanise the freaks'? (Snyder and Mitchell 2001: 380).

Disability culture

Is there a distinctive disabled people's culture? Lois Bragg (cited in Peters 2000: 584) answers 'no' on the grounds that disabled people's claim fails to meet the qualifying conditions of a common language, a historical lineage, cohesion, political solidarity, acculturation from an early age, generational/genetic links, and pride in difference. She is not the first to identify Deaf Culture as the sole exception: 'The D/deaf community apart, there is no unifying culture, language or set of experiences; people with disabilities are not homogeneous, nor is there much prospect for trans-disability solidarity' (Bickenbach 1999: 106). In complete contrast, Simi Linton argues that disabled people in America have 'solidified' as a group.

> We are everywhere these days, wheeling and loping down the street, tapping our canes, sucking on our breathing tubes, following our guide dogs, puffing and sipping on the mouth sticks that propel our motorised chairs. We may drool, hear voices, speak in staccato syllables, wear catheters to collect our urine, or live with a compromised immune system. We are all bound together, not by this list of our collective symptoms but by the social and political circumstances that have forged us as a group. (Linton 1998: 4)

Susan Peters similarly argues that disability culture is alive and vibrant. It is held together by shared values of 'radical democracy and self-empowerment' as well as 'identity, voice, justice and equality' (Peters 2000: 593). And, contra the doubters, disability culture demonstrates commonalities in historical/linguistic terms, by a commitment to social/political issues and changes, and through its personal/aesthetic values. Concerns that the emphasis on 'difference' will thwart a coherent and unifying culture are rejected on the grounds that difference is a source of strength and allows people to generate new forms of solidarity (Peters 2000).

Disability culture presumes a sense of common identity and interests that unite disabled people and separate them from their non-disabled counterparts. The exact bases for group cohesion and consciousness will vary, as will the level and form of any engagement in cultural activities. This division between 'insiders' and 'outsiders' is developed and maintained by specific cultural styles, customs and social interaction, such as in segregated, residential schooling, or by a distinctive set of experiences. There is a further presumption that a disability culture rejects the notion of impairment difference as a symbol of shame, and stresses instead solidarity and a positive identification. At the same time, a general disability culture may be contrasted with subcultures located around specific impairment groups. Furthermore, because most disabled people acquired their impairment in later life, their embrace of disability culture is inhibited by their previous immersion in a non-disabled environment.

Whatever one's conclusion regarding this debate, further questions remain about the value or possibility of a separate cultural identity:

> Firstly, there is a great deal of uncertainty amongst disabled people whether we do want 'our own culture'. After all, we all have had the experiences of resisting being treated as different, as inferior to the rest of society. So why now, when there is much greater awareness of our desire to be fully integrated into society do we suddenly want to go off at a tangent and start trying to promote our differences, our separate identity? Secondly, at this time, even if we do want to promote our own identity, our own culture, there has been precious little opportunity for us to develop a cultural life. (Finkelstein, quoted in Campbell and Oliver 1996: 111)

Historically, embryonic disability communities take form among those segregated together on the basis of their impairments. With the growth of industrialization and urbanism, the resort to specialized institutions for the most severely impaired or 'threatening' individuals expanded significantly across North America and Britain (Parker 1988). For the disabled inmates, the shared experiences in such areas as schooling and rehabilitation agencies raised the potential for developing a shared, albeit 'defensive', consciousness that sowed the seeds of a more critical and proactive disability culture (Hunt 1966a).

From the 1960s, amidst gathering forms of social protest, residential institutions provided a fertile seed-bed for developing a collective identity. The emergence of the Independent Living Movement in the USA was further stimulated by the mobilization of disabled veterans from the Vietnam War. In Britain, disabled people's campaigns can be traced back to action by a group of disabled residents at the *Le Court* Cheshire Home in Hampshire. These early years were taken up with identifying common interests and grievances and alternative ways forward (Campbell and Oliver 1996).

The crucial move in developing a disability consciousness has been the critique of disability as an individual problem that requires individual (mainly medical) solutions. One of the key mechanisms through which personal consciousness may be transformed into a collective awareness is by sharing experiences with other people in similar situations through small group meetings, books, poetry and the like (Campling 1981; Campbell and Oliver 1996). Since the 1970s, there has been a steady growth in disabled people's writings, including the appearance of an 'alternative' disability press, such as *Disability Rag*, the unofficial newspaper of the American Independent Living Movement, which began publication in 1980, and *Mouth* (Davis 1995; Brown 1997). Such initiatives sensitized a growing number of disabled people to the commonalities of disability.

Disabled people have also emulated other oppressed groups in appropriating disablist imagery, with claims of building or celebrating a 'crip culture'. Just as humour is widely used to demean disabled people, so too it is employed by disabled people to generate 'insider' recognition and solidarity, by identifying common enemies and interests, and providing a bond of 'crip humour' to disabled people's culture (Shakespeare 1994).

Increased political activism led to new representations of disabled people as active participants in protests against inaccessible buildings and transport, and welfare benefit cuts;

charity events such as Telethons as well as a broad range of campaigns for civil rights. These included disabled people chaining themselves to buses and trains, blocking roads, and crawling along the streets (Pointon 1999). In Britain, the Direct Action Network (DAN) has been in the vanguard of militant, high-profile protest actions outside Government offices, on the streets, on public transport, 'sticking two fingers up at the traditional charity-campaign image of disabled people as quietly respectable, submissive types' (Daniel 1998: 22).

This contrasted starkly with news media portrayals of disabled people as embroiled within a personal tragedy, and courageously struggling against the odds. Initially, newspapers and TV were bemused and uncertain about what to do. References to the 'last civil rights battle' were mixed with concerns that disability protest threatened to alienate supporters, or that acceding to the protesters' demands for an accessible environment was simply too expensive to contemplate. The broadsheet the *Sunday Telegraph* included a condemnation of 'the furious Quasimodos' who had engaged in a 'red paint' demonstration in Downing Street (Wilson 1997).

Deaf culture

The process of exclusion has been fundamental to the development of Deaf culture. It has its roots in the eighteenth century and the changing perception of 'Deafness' (Davis 1995). Until that time, Deaf people were excluded from the aural culture, isolated from each other, and lacked a shared, complex means of communication.

Growing urbanization encouraged Deaf people to congregate in specific areas. Everyday social interaction with other Deaf people stimulated the growth of sign language as a means of communication. This is illustrated in the growth of a Deaf community in Paris in the second half of the eighteenth century (Lane 1989), and in North America, revealed in Nora Groce's study *Everyone Here Speaks Sign Language: Hereditary D/deafness in Martha's Vineyard* (1985). In this island off Cape Cod, Massachusetts, a relatively high proportion of the island's population in the nineteenth century were Deaf, sign language users; but, most significantly, signing was learned by a significant proportion of the rest of population. Groce quotes the comments of a *Boston Sunday Herald* reporter in 1895: 'The kindly and well-informed people whom I saw, strange to say, seem to be proud of the affliction – to regard it as a kind of plume in the hat of the stock. Elsewhere the afflicted are screened as much as possible from public notoriety' (Groce 1985: 51). The assumption is that the Deaf minority was relatively well integrated into the 'normal' life of the community. More often, Deaf people have been insulated from exclusion by non-disabled culture by relying on a 'camaraderie' with like others in ways that have been 'historically created and actively transmitted across generations' (Padden and Humphries 1988: 2).

However, in seeking to understand the cultural experience of Deafness, it is necessary to distinguish between people with a hearing impairment – who may be described as deaf, or hard of hearing – who have often acquired or developed hearing loss, and are not native users of British Sign Language (BSL), and people with congenital hearing impairment who have been immersed in a BSL environment (whether at home with Deaf parents or by attending a Deaf school), and who define themselves as Deaf. It is the latter group that constitutes the members of a Deaf culture that is located in a distinctive, shared language. In addition, the community may also comprise certain hearing people, such as the children of Deaf adults who have grown up with sign language and other aspects of Deaf culture (Davis 1995).

Many Deaf people explicitly refer to themselves as a linguistic and cultural minority, making the analogy with minority ethnic groups, who are similarly likely to be excluded because they lack fluency in the dominant language. This goes with a resistance to being identified as disabled people or people with impairments (Lane 1995). It is also manifested in opposition to medical solutions, such as cochlea implants, that may restore some hearing function, and genetic screening to identify for termination of a foetus with a likely hearing impairment.

In their struggles to avoid assimilation within an 'oralist' culture and to retain their separate cultural identity, the Deaf community supports special Deaf schools as bastions of Deaf culture generally, and more specifically for their emphasis on teaching and learning through the medium of British Sign Language (BSL):

> Basically D/deaf people whose first language is BSL should be seen as a linguistic minority . . . our schools go back to the 1790s and our clubs to the 1820s. Our language is much older. D/deaf people marry each other 90% of the time, 10% have D/deaf children. Our customs and traditions have been passed down the ages and these, together with our values and beliefs, constitute our culture . . . the whole definition of culture is so much wider than the one the disability movement is espousing. (Ladd, quoted in Campbell and Oliver 1996: 120)

While there are those with a hearing impairment who do not identify in the same way with Deaf culture, it is only a minority who see themselves as part of the broader disabled population and disability culture (Corker 1998a). This reflects the uneasy 'stand-off' between Deaf people and organizations of disabled people that has often inhibited joint political action.

Disability arts

Disability culture is built on the premiss that there is a moral and political obligation to celebrate difference. The emergence of a disability arts movement marks a significant stage in the transition to a positive portrayal of disabled people, and a sure sign of its political awakening: 'disability arts would not have been possible without disability politics coming along first. It's what makes a disability artist different from an artist with a disability' (Sutherland 1997: 159).

The disability arts movement encompasses several, re-inforcing dimensions. First, it argues for disabled people to have access to the mainstream of artistic consumption and production. Second, it explores the experience of living with an impairment. Third, and most crucially, disability arts offer a critical response to the experience of social exclusion and marginalization. It entails using culture and the media to expose the discrimination and prejudice that disabled people face, and to generate a positive group consciousness and identity (Barnes et al. 1999). Nonetheless, there remains a crucial distinction between 'disabled people doing art' and 'disability arts', which is more overtly 'political'.

Disability arts are potentially educative, expressive and transformative. They emphasize the potential of cultural action as a progressive, emancipatory force at both individual and social levels. The focus on oppression and injustice provides the rationale for a diverse array of cultural interventions in which subversive representations or performances illuminate and confront discriminatory barriers and attitudes. Where the audience is primarily non-disabled people, some disabled artists adopt a deliberate tactic of 'outing' impairment, often their own, in an attempt to counter social conventions that impairment is something best kept hidden. For some the shock value of a public display of impairment is a first stage in making a non-disabled audience feel guilty for experiencing revulsion. At the same time, there is an uncertain boundary line between challenging disability and encouraging voyeurism or pathologizing impairment.

By contrast, traditional paternalistic approaches believe that disabled people are incapable of communicating their thoughts and feelings through the arts, except perhaps as a means of individual therapy or part of a process of rehabilitation. This view has pervaded the activities promoted within special schools, day centres and segregated institutions. These tend to depoliticize creativity, although they are instead exploited for commercial purposes, such as charity Christmas cards. While there is a place for art therapy, disabled people have increasingly developed a more reflective and active orientation: 'Introducing disabled people to the social role of artistic creativity and opening a debate about disability culture is a dynamic way of assisting disabled people to challenge their assumed dependency and place in mainstream society' (Morrison and Finkelstein 1993: 127).

In North America, the emergence of a disability consciousness may be traced through the 1960s and 1970s (Bowe 1978). Autobiographical accounts flourished, and while most reflected a standard 'living with my impairment' approach, there were notable exceptions, such as Irving Zola's (1982) story of his personal and intellectual journey in rethinking disability and identity. This American and Canadian literature was extended with an increasing production of novels, comedy, songs, poetry, drama, paintings and sculpture. These conveyed an emerging sense of group identity and interests (Saxton and Howe 1988; Davis 1995; Hirsch 1995; Tremain 1996). These contributions flowered as a complement to disability rights protests, so that by the early 1990s a distinctive 'Disability Culture Movement' had been identified (Shapiro 1993; Longmore 1995; Brown 1997).

Parallel trends in Britain include the first production of a television programme in 1975 specifically for (and increasingly produced by) disabled people, entitled *Link*, and the production of a range of newsletters and magazines by disabled people and groups. This has included a remarkable growth in contributions from disabled poets, musicians, artists and entertainers (Morrison and Finkelstein 1993). *In From the Cold*, the magazine produced by Britain's Liberation Network of Disabled People, appeared between 1981 and 1987. *Coalition*, the magazine of the Greater Manchester Coalition of Disabled People (GMCDP), was first published in 1986 and is still going strong; while *DAIL* (Disability Arts in London) Magazine has been running since 1987. The number of conferences, exhibitions, workshops, cabarets and performances has also continued apace (Pointon and Davies 1997). By the late 1980s, a number of 'specialist' disability programmes were being transmitted on British television, and in 1993 the British Broadcasting Corporation set up the Disability Programmes Unit, staffed mainly by disabled people, that promoted a critical awareness of disability issues.

There has been increased recognition of the importance of involving disabled people in mainstream culture. In the USA, The Americans with Disabilities Act (ADA), for example, forced suppliers of television sets to build in a decoder chip so that D/deaf people could receive the 'closed caption' (a type of subtitling) system for viewers with hearing impairments. In the UK, National Lottery funding was awarded to the Royal School for the Deaf to help build Europe's sign language video library – the first phase of a £1 million National Sign Language Video Centre.

The disability arts movement is important in that it provides space for a critical reflection on ways to empowerment (Morrison and Finkelstein 1993). Nevertheless, there are uncertainties about its reflection of difference, and whether disability art and culture will be assimilated into mainstream culture and neutralized.

Review

Analyses of cultural domination or 'imperialism' have highlighted the dominance of disabling images across the range of modern media. Historically, disabling imagery has reinforced the social exclusion and oppression of disabled people. Until recently, it has been specific impairment groups, rather than disabled people generally, who have forged a common identity. The disabled population is scattered, isolated and divided, rather than a cohesive, self-conscious 'community'. There have been too few organizations controlled by disabled people promoting their own interests. The multiple experiences and identities among disabled people also inhibit collective mobilization and identification. However, a disability culture is emerging. Disabled people are becoming politicized and aware of their collective interests. This sets the scene for a struggle by disabled people to supplant oppressive media and cultural representations with others that reflect their own experiences and values. It heralds the generation of a disability culture that expresses and sustains a positive disabled identity.

A similar struggle has been under way with respect to disabled people's exclusion from political institutions and processes. In chapter 6, we discuss how political domination is exercised, and how disabled people are fighting back and attempting to redefine disability politics.

6

The Politics of Disability: Breaking Down the Barriers?

A key factor in explaining the transformation of the concept 'disability' from an individual medical problem to a socio-political issue has been the extraordinary politicization of disabled people since the 1960s. It has generated campaigns at local, national and international levels. This is further associated with the emergence of a positive disabled people's culture and identity.

In this chapter, we review the involvement of disabled people across the range of politics, from participation in 'conventional' political processes and institutions, such as elections, legislatures and the courts, to other forms of political organization and protest for radical social change. We examine a central claim in the disability literature that disabled people have been marginalized from the liberal democratic political process, thus reinforcing wider experiences of 'powerlessness'. In practice, people's experiences and responses are more complex, because of the additional impact of other oppressions such as 'race', gender, sexuality and age. Illustrations are provided of the development of campaigns for anti-discrimination legislation and the focus of citizenship and civil rights. We also examine arguments that a more radical and innovative form of disability politics took hold in the last quarter of the twentieth century. This linked disabled people's protests with 'new social movements', but signalled a tension between building a politics of distribution and one of affirmation (Fraser 1995; Young 1997).

Liberal democratic politics

The defining mantra of liberal democratic societies is 'government of the people, by the people, for the people'. In practice, this means periodic elections for legislative bodies, with 'regular' opportunities to influence elected representatives and political parties through individual contact, pressure groups and public campaigns. Even this implies a degree of public involvement that is rarely achieved. In practice, political power and influence are distributed unevenly, with some (dominant) groups better placed to secure their interests. While the use of overt political force and control through 'repressive' state institutions is always an option, the key to social stability is the consensual legitimation of power. The achievement of willing consent or ideological hegemony (Gramsci 1971, 1985) and the importance of discourse through power/knowledge relations (Foucault 1980) reflect the political importance of a diverse range of institutional contexts, such as schools, the mass media and established religions.

Elections and voting

One of the most basic rights in a democratic society is participation in the political process. Yet in many countries disabled people face barriers when attempting to exercise the right to vote. In Britain, it was not until The Representation of the People Act in 1983 that those labelled as having a 'mental illness' and living in institutions were allowed to be put on the electoral register, and then only under stringent conditions that were not repealed until the Act was revised in 2000. However, people with learning difficulties have had to make do with less positive action (Scott and Morris 2001). Similarly, in Australia, 'many people with intellectual and psychiatric disabilities, especially those who are homeless or institutionalised, experience *de facto* disenfranchisement through never being entered on electoral rolls' (Davis 1999: 70). Often, other family members have omitted disabled members from the electoral register because of low or mistaken assumptions about their capacity to exercise their vote (Lamb and Layzell 1994).

In addition, access issues pose particular problems for disabled people wishing to vote or to participate in political meetings. Relevant political information from political parties is rarely produced in accessible formats such as Braille, tape or video (Enticott et al. 1992; Scott and Morris 2001). Voting difficulties include transport, access to polling stations, and marking ballot papers. In the 2001 British General Election, access problems were reported at 69 per cent of polling stations, although this had fallen from 88 per cent in 1992 (Scott and Morris 2001). The Representation of the People Act 2000 required access to tactile templates and large-print ballot papers, but these were not available in more than a third of polling stations (Scott and Morris 2001). There is the possibility of voting by post or by proxy, but this is often a daunting, bureaucratic process, aside from the obvious drawback that votes must be cast before the election campaign is over.

Parallel concerns have been expressed in the USA, where confusion in counting ballot papers in Florida during the 2000 Presidential election highlighted the significant barriers confronting groups of disabled people in recording their votes. This followed legal action against the New York City government by Disabled in Action over inaccessible polling stations. These deficiencies are replicated in many other countries, where disabled people's involvement in the democratic process is made dependent on relatives, friends and personal assistants (Enticott et al. 1992).

Parties and pressure groups

Further barriers exist for disabled people wishing to enter party politics. 'Deaf and dumb persons' were declared ineligible for election to the British Parliament as recently as 1955 (Drake 1999). Although this restriction has been overturned, political parties remain even more reticent to select disabled candidates than to select females or those from minority ethnic communities. Moreover, those disabled people who are elected rarely identify with disability issues. This reflects a general lack of interest in disability politics. In the 1997 British General Election, 'neither of the (main) parties, the candidates, election material nor the media paid significant attention to issues that may affect disabled people' (Christie with Mensah-Coker 1999: 67).

Single-issue pressure group lobbying and campaigns provides a further avenue for political action. There are now hundreds of organizations, varying widely in membership, seeking to influence the different levels of government. In liberal democratic societies, pressure groups with the most political clout are the more established 'corporate groups', such as employers' federations, private businesses, professional associations and, to a lesser degree, trade unions. There is also another, more pluralistic world of 'competing interest groups' drawn in from the voluntary sector (Cawson 1982). Since they have a less crucial role in the economy, they tend to have little political influence. Groups concerned with disability tend to fit this last category.

However, there are significant differences between organizations in their objectives, leadership and membership. Aside from umbrella or co-ordinating organizations such as Disabled People's International (DPI), the American Coalition of Citizens with Disabilities (ACCD), and the British Council of Disabled People (BCODP), the following categories may be identified:

1. Charities/patronage These are traditional organizations and charities run and controlled by non-disabled people *for* disabled people. They often provide impairment-related services for disabled people, carers and professionals, often in conjunction with statutory agencies and professional bodies.

2. Single-issue These may be organizations *for* or *of* disabled people. The latter are organizations controlled and run by disabled people themselves. They focus on single issues and/or lobby for particular sections of the disabled population. Examples include the American Foundation for the

Blind and, in Britain, the Disablement Income Group and the Disability Alliance.

3. *Self-help/activist*   These are organizations *of* disabled people. They include grass-roots self-help projects, campaigning and advocacy groups, as well as national organizations. They may work alone or in collaboration with other local or national voluntary agencies. This category includes various Centres for Independent Living (CILs) in America, and equivalents in Britain, as well as some impairment-specific groups such as the Spinal Injuries Association. A more 'activist' approach stresses user control, collective political action, and consciousness raising. Examples include the Union of the Physically Impaired Against Segregation (UPIAS), the British Deaf Association (BDA), and Americans Disabled for Attendant Programs Today (ADAPT).

Until the 1980s, charities and single-issue lobby groups *for* disabled people dominated the disability field (Oliver 1990). Within disability politics, most adhered to a traditional individualistic medical approach, and were often under the control of parents of disabled people or professionals. Activities ranged from information services, mutual support, social events and fund-raising to building close working relationships with politicians and policy makers that gave them a degree of political credibility and influence (Barnes 1991). In the UK, there are economic advantages, such as tax concessions, for organizations that adopt a charitable status. However, it is illegal for the 'beneficiaries' of such organizations to be members of their management boards or committees, or for charities to be openly involved in political campaigns. As a consequence, they are largely dominated by non-disabled officers and offer little scope for disabled people's empowerment (Drake 1996).

An illustration of single-issue pressure group activity in Britain is the Disablement Income Group (DIG) formed in 1965 by two disabled women (Megan du Boisson and Berit Moore) to campaign for a national disability income. Poverty was a major concern for disabled people in the 1960s, and DIG lobbied Parliament and organized demonstrations (Campbell and Oliver 1996). In the following decade, fifty voluntary groups formed a larger umbrella organization known as the Disability Alliance (DA), and produced a regular flow of reports documenting the link between impairment and poverty and the case for a national disability income. More usually, however, single-issue groups have concentrated on impairment-specific concerns.

Practical schemes with a 'self-help' philosophy designed to enhance the control of disabled people over their lives have multiplied in recent years. For example, disabled people identified lack of information as a major obstacle to developing new services. This led to the establishment of the Disability Information and Advice Line (DIAL), with local groups being established around Britain: 'DIAL not only contributed to the breakdown in the knowledge monopoly held by professional disability experts but also gave disabled people a deeper sense of the increased choices possible for those wanting to live independently in their own homes in the community' (Finkelstein 1993b: 39).

These moves towards self-organization and public displays of defiance were an empowering process for many disabled people:

> This vocabulary of protest marks a significant shift in consciousness from one of almost passive dependence to active involvement in raising that consciousness to the point where the minority group is no longer one for whom pleas, reforms and changes are made by others but where they themselves are instrumental in provoking change. (D. Thomas 1982: 189)

The self-help approach has been increasingly associated with the expansion of user-led voluntary organizations. The pressure for user-led services emerges not simply from dissatisfaction with traditional provider-led models of service delivery, which exhibit low standards and accountability, but has been stimulated by the growing emphasis on citizenship rights (Croft and Beresford 1992). A basic distinction is often drawn between two main organizational models – consumerist and democratic – on the basis of the level and form of participation expected of disabled people. The consumerist approach highlights the role of disabled people as customers, while the democratic model promotes user-led, if not controlled, organizations (Robson et al. 1997).

In addition to usual concerns about resources and the education and training of staff, there is often uncertainty about whether such organizations can pursue both a service provider and a campaigning role (Stalker et al. 1999). In America, CILs in the 1970s were in the vanguard of disability politics, whereas by the 1990s they had become more 'neutral' service providers:

> Most CILs do not hire politically active people, do not have organisers, and have no strategic view of how to effect social change. Many executive directors of CILs and disability rights groups are apolitical, outside narrowly defined disability related issues. Most disability rights groups avoid demonstrations because they are considered outdated, or because they would alienate funding sources. (Charlton 1998: 122)

Civil rights and anti-discrimination legislation

The political participation of disabled people and their organizations opened up a 'new front' in the area of civil rights and anti-discrimination legislation. This highlights important contrasts between North American and European political contexts and disabled people's struggles. The ideological cornerstones of American society – market capitalism, consumer sovereignty, self-reliance, and economic and political freedom – were replicated in the approach of the Independent Living Movement (ILM). It stressed civil rights, consumerism, self-help, de-medicalization, and deinstitutionalization (DeJong 1979). The ILM opposed the professionally dominated and bureaucratic provision of social welfare services, and their sparseness, while demanding opportunities for disabled people to develop their own services in the marketplace.

When the first CIL was set up in 1972 in Berkeley, California, the initiative was taken by disabled university students housed by the university authorities in a local hospital 'for their own good'. Led by Ed Roberts, they rejected this custodial environment and sought a community 'home' where supportive services were provided. The CIL adhered to three guiding principles: disabled people were best qualified to determine their needs and how these should be met; a comprehensive programme of support was required; and disabled people should be integrated as fully as possible into their community (Centre for Independent Living 1982: 250–1). More generally, the ILM advocated distinctive approaches to traditional rehabilitation services in terms of their aims, methods of delivery, and programme management (Cole 1979). Client choice and control were accentuated, with peer counselling highlighted and personal care directed by the disabled person, in contrast to traditional professionally dominated modes.

In European countries, the strategic priority has been to enhance existing State-sponsored welfare systems to meet disabled people's needs. The Welfare State is regarded as essential to overcome the perceived shortcomings of market provision and heightened barriers experienced by poorer disabled people. By contrast, the ILM's approach meant that some groups such as young, white Americans with physical and sensory impairments were better placed to exploit the possibilities of market competition (Blaxter 1984; Williams 1984b).

In Britain, organizations of disabled people mobilized opinion initially against their traditional categorization as a vulnerable group in need of 'care'. They argued for the right to define their own needs and service priorities and against traditional service-provider domination. Most notably, the Derbyshire Coalition of Disabled People drew up its own list of seven fundamental needs of disabled people: 'information, access, housing, technical aids, personal assistance, counselling and transport', which exerted considerable influence in the growth of independent living initiatives across the country (Davis and Mullender 1993).

With a growing impact on the choice of strategies and priorities for the advancement of disabled people's interests has been the struggles around 'rights'. According to T. H. Marshall (1950), civil, political and social rights constitute the basis of modern citizenship. The civil rights emphasis in disability politics took off first in the USA, where there has been a long tradition of rights-based political campaigns. These were given considerable reinforcement in the Civil Rights struggles of the 1960s, which in turn influenced the activities of disabled people's organizations. The American

black civil rights struggles, with their combination of conventional lobbying tactics and mass political action, provided
a major stimulus to an emerging 'disability rights movement' (Hahn 1987; Shapiro 1993). By contrast, the disabled
people's movement in Britain has concentrated on achieving
changes in social policy, or a legislative route. Without a
written constitution, or human rights legislation (until 1998),
and with greater involvement of national charities in lobbying for 'progressive' legislation as compared with the United
States, protest campaigns were constrained to follow different
political paths (Imrie and Wells 1993).

Until the mid-1970s, the disability rights movement was a
loosely structured amalgam of grass-roots groups and organizations. For example, Disabled in Action was formed in
New York in 1970 with the sole purpose of engaging in
political campaigns (Scotch 1988). It adopted direct action,
with demonstrations, sit-ins and protests particularly prominent (Shapiro 1993). Lobbying within Congress also gathered
momentum. Sympathetic legislators in key posts helped insert
disability-related provisions into the 1973 Rehabilitation Act.
Section 504 is particularly important because, for the first
time, it prohibited discrimination against disabled people in
any federally funded programme. The Act also promoted
environmental access, more comprehensive services, employment opportunities, and an increase in the numbers of CILs.
'The enactment of Section 504 was brought about largely by
the activism of disabled people themselves. A number of
sit-ins took place before the appropriate regulations were
finally issued. The militancy of these sit-ins . . . vividly con-
tradicted the stereotype of the disabled person as powerless'
(Zola 1983: 56).

However, local, state and federal governments were reluctant to implement Section 504, and this generated further
action. A key role was played by the American Coalition of
Citizens with Disabilities (ACCD), formed in 1974, with
growing tension between those aiming to effect policy change
at federal and state levels and those concentrating on grass-
roots initiatives (Scotch 1988; Zola 1994). At the same time,
there was increased resort to legal battles involving disabled
individuals seeking redress for the denial of their constitu-
tional rights. This attracted considerable media attention, and

heightened public awareness of the struggles for disabled people's rights. It eventually culminated in the Americans with Disabilities Act (ADA) 1990 – the oldest and most comprehensive anti-discrimination legislation in the world (Doyle 1999).

The ADA's formal objective was to 'mainstream' disabled Americans as fully as was 'practicable'. It outlawed discrimination against disabled people in employment, transport and the built environment, state and local government, and telecommunications (Pfeiffer 1994). However, there were immediate concerns that the Act supported traditional analyses and solutions: 'with its culture of individualism, absolute individual rights and a rejection of paternalistic state agencies, the analysis has incorporated individualistic objectives of anti-dependency, empowerment and economic self-sufficiency through remunerative employment' (Bickenbach 1999: 105).

It has encouraged notable improvements in the accessibility of the built environment, but its effects in other areas have been much less than anticipated. The independent National Council on Disability in its examination of the enforcement activities found that

> while the Administration has consistently asserted its strong support for the civil rights of people with disabilities, the federal agencies charged with the enforcement and policy development under ADA have, to varying degrees, been underfunded, overly cautious, reactive and lacking any coherent and unifying national strategy. In addition, enforcement agencies have not consistently taken leadership roles in clarifying 'frontier' or emergent issues. (Bristo 2000: 1)

Specific concerns have been expressed about its slowness, the weaknesses of its monitoring and enforcement provisions, and its impact on minority groups within the disabled population. Moreover, the onus is on the disabled person to seek 'reasonable accommodation'. In practice, the overwhelming majority of cases are settled out of court, with 95 per cent of the remainder decided in favour of the employer (National Council on Disability 2000b).

Nevertheless, its passage symbolized a significant shift in the perception of disabled people within the United States, and acted as a beacon to anti-discrimination legislation in other countries through the 1990s, including the Australian Disability Discrimination Act (1992), the inclusion of disability discrimination within a Human Rights Act in New Zealand in 1993, and the Disability Discrimination Act (1995) in Britain (Doyle 1999). Not to be outdone, Canada included disability as a category entitled to human rights in the Canadian Charter of Rights and Freedoms in 1985.

Since the 1970s, British organizations controlled and run by disabled people, such as the UPIAS, the Liberation Network, and Sisters Against Disability (SAD), have embraced similar goals to their American counterparts, with the pursuit of disabled people's rights at centre stage, but with signs of increasing readiness to take legal action. A key element in these campaigns was the establishment of the Committee on Restrictions Against Disabled People (CORAD) by the Labour Government in 1978. This led to a recommendation for legislative action (Barnes et al. 1999), but Margaret Thatcher's newly elected Conservative Government proved far less sympathetic. It was left to Jack Ashley, a deaf Labour MP, to introduce a private member's anti-discrimination bill in July 1982, but it was not successful.

However, the campaign for an anti-discrimination law continued. In 1985 the Voluntary Organizations for Anti-Discrimination Legislation (VOADL) Committee – renamed Rights Now in 1992 – was established. This provided an uneasy alliance between organizations controlled and run by disabled people and more traditional organizations for disabled people that had often been lukewarm about civil rights legislation for disabled people. At the same time, this was also a period of growing politicization among disabled people. A key factor was the surge in Disability Equality Training (DET) – an approach to consciousness raising based on the social model of disability (Oliver and Barnes 1998). By the mid-1990s, all the major political parties acknowledged the need for legislation, and the Conservative Government introduced a bill in 1994 that was enacted as the Disability Discrimination Act (DDA) 1995.

As with the ADA, Britain's Disability Discrimination Act is based on an individual, medical approach. The individual complainant must prove that they have an impairment before litigation can begin. The Act defines discrimination as arising in instances of 'less favourable treatment' without good cause, and where reasonable adjustments are not made. The law provides only limited protection from direct discrimination in employment, the provision of goods and services, and in the selling or letting of land. Initially, education and transport were excluded from its provisions. Over 90 per cent of employers were not covered by the Act because they employed fewer than twenty people (Doyle 1999; Gooding 2000). In practice, as of 1999, most cases (74 per cent) were withdrawn or settled before a full tribunal hearing, while a further 10 per cent were dismissed (Meager et al. 1999).

Informed business commentators in Britain expressed alarm that disability rights legislation imposed a financial burden unlike comparable initiatives: 'outlawing discrimination against blacks or women does not cost anything, but outlawing discrimination against disabled people will often involve costs' (*Economist* 1994). The DDA began life without an enforcement agency to monitor its implementation. This is in marked contrast to the ADA and even other British anti-discrimination legislation such as the 1975 Sex Discrimination Act (SDA), with its Equal Opportunities Commission (EOC), and the 1976 Race Relations Act (RRA), with the Commission for Racial Equality (CRE). Yet such bodies have been only marginally effective in combating discrimination. Although formally 'independent', funding and appointments to the EOC and CRE are subject to political constraints. As a result, the bulk of their activities have centred on 'education and research', rather than enforcement or addressing structural disadvantages (Bagilhole 1997).

The New Labour Government set up a Disability Rights Taskforce after its election in 1997 and, following its recommendations and intense lobbying, it set up the Disability Rights Commission (DRC) in April 2000 to facilitate 'the elimination of discrimination against disabled people'. The DRC has the power to take up cases on behalf of individuals and organizations. Early indications suggest that, like the EOC and the CRE, its main activities will span the production of new codes of practice, the updating of existing ones, the provision of information and advice, conciliation and research.

At another political level, the European Commission adopted a directive on equal opportunities for disabled people in 1996. This encouraged (not required) member states to abandon segregated facilities in favour of mainstreaming for disabled people. In addition, a clause to counter discrimination against various groups including disabled people was written into the revised Treaty of the European Union in 1997 (Sayce 2000: 182). The European Union in October 2000 agreed to a directive requiring member states to introduce anti-discrimination legislation in a number of areas, including disability, and 2003 has been declared the European Year of Disabled Citizens.

The passage of the Human Rights Act 1998, as well as the impact of European Community law, promises a further significant impact on UK disability politics that may yet lead to the British disabled people's movement moving closer to the profile adopted by its counterparts in Australia and New Zealand, with campaigns for increased civil rights as well as fundamental social changes. It is likely to encourage individual actions and impact on rights to privacy and family life, but may have further far-reaching implications if, for example, the courts pronounce on the human rights of a person with learning difficulties. By contrast, the DRC cannot pursue human rights cases. There was also international-level pressure, with agreement on the United Nations *Standard Rules on the Equalization of Opportunities for Persons with Disabilities* (United Nations 1993), which outlined a radical programme for governments to follow in the area of disability rights (see chapter 7).

Yet, despite considerable enthusiasm among disabled people's groups on both sides of the Atlantic, there is also criticism that the legal route leads to long, drawn-out, costly court actions that downgrade collective political struggles, and ignore the social and political location of the legal system. In addition,

A rights-based approach to legal development has been rejected by many modern critical legal scholars. They raise a number of concerns about rights. These include a misuse and abuse of the concept of rights; the indeterminism of rights; the fact that rights are unstable and context bound; the fact that rights cannot determine consequences; and the fact that rights formalise relationships and thereby separate us from each other. (Jones and Marks 1999: 22)

Towards a new social movement?

While conventional politics remains central to political campaigns by disabled people and their organizations, the failures of pressure group and electoral politics to win significant policy reforms have encouraged a more radical disability politics. This has given rise to suggestions that the disabled people's movement may lay claim to being a 'new social movement' (NSM) (Oliver 1990, 1996c), or a 'liberation struggle' (Shakespeare 1993).

Historic hopes in the revolutionary potential of the industrial working class were dashed by its incorporation into welfare capitalism. Some writers on the Left transferred their hopes for progressive social change to a burgeoning range of new protest movements emerging in the 1970s and 1980s that included the women's movement and peace and environmental groups (Touraine 1981; A. Scott 1990). Yet the defining features of NSMs were a source of intense debate. Some commentators stressed their capacity to resist bureaucratic encroachment (Melucci 1989), along with their expressive politics and allegiance to more direct forms of democracy (Habermas 1981). Others queried the claimed disjuncture between 'old'- and 'new'-style politics and protest. There are, for example, close parallels between the women's suffrage movement of the early twentieth century and more recent feminist struggles (Shakespeare 1993). Indeed, the roots of disability protest lie at least in the early decades of the twentieth century. Low pay and poor working conditions prompted the National League of the Blind and the Disabled (NLBD) to mobilize blind workers from around Britain to march to London in 1920, and the NLBD also campaigned against the policies of charities, thereby triggering protest marches in the 1930s and 1940s (Pagel 1988). A similar engagement in political action occurred in the United States over this period (Longmore and Goldberger 2000).

Nevertheless, in his review of the disabled people's movement's claims to NSM status, Oliver (1990) adopts a positive response based on the following criteria: that it is (i) peripheral to conventional politics; (ii) offers a critical evaluation of society; (iii) embraces 'post-materialist' or 'post-acquisitive' values; and (iv) adopts an international perspective (Oliver 1996c). While these are open to very different interpretations, this list omits the widely noted association between NSMs and the 'new middle class' (Touraine 1981; A. Scott 1990), and arguments by others that they involve a 'celebration of difference' (Young 1990). There is nevertheless a wider agreement that major realignments in capitalism had paved the way for new political groupings, based on changing lines of social division and conflict, as well as stimulated by the social and cultural dynamics of a post-modern society (Fagan and Lee 1997).

Peripheral to conventional politics

Until recently, there were few organizations controlled and run by disabled people, and these exercised little influence on policy makers. Traditionally, voluntary bodies and charities have dominated how disability is seen within political circles. Many are concerned only with impairment-specific issues, and increasingly with service provision, rather than direct political campaigns. Disenchantment with the impact and character of these organizations led to an unprecedented growth in campaigning, self-help and activist groups. The emphasis shifted to self-organization and a commitment to radical political action so as to influence the behaviour of groups, organizations and institutions (Anspach 1979; DeJong 1979): 'the purpose of disabled people's self-organisation is to promote change: to improve the quality of our lives and promote our full inclusion into society. It does this both through involvement in the formal political system and through promotion of other kinds of political activity' (Campbell and Oliver 1996: 22).

In Britain, the formation of the UPIAS in 1974 broke new ground. It comprised a small but influential group of disabled activists located in residential institutions who sought more control over their lives. As in the USA, such groups continue to provide an important source of ideas and support, by promoting disabled people's collective interests, both to statutory agencies and political parties, and across local and national levels (Zola 1983; National Council on Disability 2000a). A further significant development in Britain was the emergence of BCODP as a national umbrella for organizations controlled by disabled people. It had representatives from only seven national groups at its first meeting in 1981, but quickly became a national voice of disabled people in the campaign for political rights. By July 2000, membership had grown to 130 organizations representing more than 400,000 disabled people.

However, disability activists on both sides of the Atlantic expressed periodic concerns about the risk of incorporation. Even so, most disabled people's groups have taken the conventional political path, albeit with some considerable soul-searching:

> To get too close to the Government is to risk incorporation and end up carrying out their proposals rather than ours. To move too far away is to risk marginalization and eventual demise. To collaborate too eagerly with the organizations for disabled people risks having our agendas taken over by them, and having them presented both to us and to politicians as theirs. To remain aloof risks appearing unrealistic and/or unreasonable, and denies possible access to much needed resources. (Barnes and Oliver 1995: 115)

From this perspective, there has been a worrying movement of disabled activists into the mainstream of politics as governments have placed a higher priority on disability issues. This has entailed more consultation with representatives of disabled people as well as appointing disabled people to Government-sponsored organizations (Shapiro 1993).

A critical evaluation of society

New social movements define themselves in counter-hegemonic terms. A defining feature has been their focus on social oppression. The barriers to inclusion are embedded in policies and practices based on the individualistic, medical approach to disability. The removal of such obstacles involves gaining control over material resources and the range and quality of services. It requires recognition of the contribution of hostile physical and social environments to the marginalization and powerlessness experienced by disabled people. The aim is that disabled people will be 'consciously engaged in critical evaluation of capitalist society and in the creation of alternative models of social organisation at local, national and international levels, as well as trying to reconstruct the world ideologically and to create alternative forms of service provision' (Oliver 1990: 113).

Those promoting the social model have stressed its radical credentials. Concrete evidence of this is seen in the marked contrast between the traditional, voluntary, paternalistic organizations *for* disabled people of the pre-1970s and the newer, more representative organizations *of* disabled people established in the last decades of the twentieth century that were controlled by disabled people (Priestley 1999). Nevertheless, there are strong differences of interpretation around the social model, and it has been invoked in support of initiatives that are far less radical – as happened with the anti-labelling approaches to normalization and integration (Soder 1989). Hence, service provision for people with learning difficulties remains rooted in a care, protection and welfare ethos, although couched in the language of empowerment and civil rights.

A further aspect of the 'new' politics has been its adoption of unconventional political tactics, including demonstrations, direct action and civil disobedience. These attracted particular attention in the United States, where disability protests often took their cue from the actions of other social protest movements of the late 1960s and 1970s. 'When traditional legal channels have been exhausted, disabled people have learned to employ other techniques of social protest' (DeJong 1983: 12). The recent engagement in 'direct action' represents a shift in the balance from 'old'- to 'new'-style political protests and campaigning. A central objective has been to attract maximum publicity, so action is 'often carefully planned to influence opinion-formers, the media etc.' (Shakespeare 1993: 258). Through the 1990s there have been a growing number of demonstrations that present a new image of disabled people. Major demonstrations have been held in the USA and Britain against charity shows and Telethons (Longmore 1997). In Britain, this precipitated the end of such events in 1992, while also leading to the formation in 1993 of the Direct Action Network (DAN), which organized more than 200 local and national demonstrations within five years (Pointon 1999). These have posed a high-profile challenge to orthodox notions of disability and a passive disabled identity.

Disabled people's groups around the world have emulated each other's tactics and campaigns in employing direct action to invade government buildings and disrupt transportation systems and media events. In America, ADAPT has been in the vanguard of such protests, with protests outside the White House in favour of a national attendant care policy and occupation of the Federal Department of Transportation building to demand more accessible inter-city coaches. In Australia, the Prime Minister's office in Sydney was occupied in 1997 in protest against budget cuts to the Human Rights and Equal Opportunities Commission (Gleeson 1999).

Post-material values

Another feature identified as distinguishing NSMs is their adherence to 'post-materialist' or 'post-acquisitive' values. This is particularly evident with environmental and peace groups, but less so when applied generally to disabled people, or indeed women's and minority ethnic groups. The latter have been particularly concerned to overturn disadvantages in the distribution of income and wealth, and in the labour market and welfare benefit system. Indeed, the demand for more resources and service support typifies disabled people's demands around the world.

In other accounts of NSMs, a tension has been identified between what Nancy Fraser (1997a) terms a politics of 'distribution' and one of 'affirmation'. Certainly, disabled people's protest, like feminist politics, is committed to a more expressive politics that seeks social justice, empowerment and more direct forms of democracy – hence the significance of developing a cultural dimension to politics that challenges disabling stereotypes and affirms a positive disabled identity. It is in this sense that the disabled people's movement has 'gone beyond' issues of resource allocation and redistribution to critique the 'able-bodied normality' that permeates Western societies (Fagan and Lee 1997). However, this falls short of a comprehensive denial of core capitalist values.

Internationalization

Another key feature in the politicization of disability has been the international character of the disabled people's movement (Driedger 1989). Disabled activists formed Disabled People's International (DPI) in 1981. Its first world congress was held in Singapore in the following year, and attracted 400 delegates from around the world. They agreed on a common programme: the empowerment of disabled people through collective political action (DPI 1982). For DPI, the prerequisite for change lies in the promotion and nurture of grassroots organizations and the development of public awareness of disability issues. It has acted as a major catalyst for discussion of the creation and spread of impairment and disability through poverty, industrial development, pollution and war (Charlton 1998).

There has also been important sharing of experiences in developing new forms of self-organization. For example, the promotion of 'independent living' has drawn heavily on the American experience. There are now CILs or equivalent organizations across Europe and in other more industrialized countries such as Australia, Canada and Japan, as well as in South America and Africa (Charlton 1998). A further instance of the impact of the disabled people's movement at the international level is found in the attention given to disability issues within transnational organizations such as the United Nations, the International Labour Organization, and the World Health Organization (Driedger 1989). But although organization at the international level has encouraged national movements to learn from other's experiences, there is considerable variation in disability policy outcomes (see chapter 7).

Overall, the disabled people's movement demonstrates both radical and conventional sides. The balance has varied, and arguably the numbers committed to a separate NSM strategy and goals has lost ground to the clear majority who are comfortable working through established political institutions and trying to break down disabling barriers from within the system. Other disabled people move back and forth between the different types of political protest. Yet, for most disabled people, what is important is not whether the disabled people's struggle is categorized as either 'new'- or 'old'-style politics, but whether it sustains and enhances the extraordinary vitality and impact of disability politics over recent decades.

Identity politics

Initially, the politicization of disabled people was viewed as a response to their common experience of oppression. This provided a unifying group identity and interest, while identifying the source of their grievances in the structures and processes of a disabling society. For many disabled people, engaging in collective action was liberating and empowering. In this way, they openly challenged the public stereotype of their passivity and dependence. Moreover, by mobilizing against the injustices of social oppression, disabled people built on a positive definition of group differences, instead of these being regarded as signs of abnormality. Disabled people's protests represent one among several examples of a socially oppressed group asserting its 'cultural and experiential specificity' (Young 1990: 160).

Just as 'self-identity' is a central issue in considering the emergence of disability culture, so too is it at the heart of disability politics. Yet many individuals with an impairment do not 'self-identify' as disabled people, or get involved in political activity of any kind. Some American disabled writers have noted that disability politics is divided on social class grounds. Marta Russell, for example, illustrates how some of the worst effects of poverty on disabled people can be mitigated by 'class power' or, more directly, the monetary resources of individual middle-class, disabled people (Russell 1998: 131). Of course, similar comments can be applied to other contemporary social movements, but disabled people's campaigns demonstrate a marked under-representation of older people (Walker and Walker 1998), individuals from minority ethnic groups (Vernon 1999), people with learning difficulties (Chappell 1997), and mental health system users and survivors (Sayce 2000). For the disabled people's movement to continue to be an effective force for change, it must overcome the reluctance of people with a range of impairments to engage in disability politics or adopt a 'disabled identity'.

However, while disabled activists were promoting a group identity culture and politics, they found themselves increasingly challenged by the transition to an identity politics that became a 'celebration of difference' (Woodward 1997). Now, the emphasis on a disabled identity was criticized for being in conflict with a truly emancipatory politics. Indeed, no limits were placed on the amount of difference or the distinct collectivities that might emerge, in terms of age, gender, 'race' and sexuality, for example, to undercut the claims of a common, disabled group identity. Any political movement based on the notion of identity found itself exposed to charges that it denied 'difference' and was liable to fracture. As the disabled people's movement had already discovered with respect to Deaf people, disabled identities are sometimes contested; but now they were interpreted as altogether more uncertain, fluid and lacking any firm base.

For critics of this 'politics of identity', such as Nancy Fraser (1995, 1997a, 1997b), it signalled a retreat from a vision of a 'just social order', and a shift away from struggles over redistribution to focus on winning 'recognition' of social collectivities in a distinctive cultural political struggle. She argues that, whatever its claims, an essentially 'cultural politics of identity and difference' fails to connect with a 'social politics of justice and equality' (1997a: 186). For the millions of people in the world experiencing extreme poverty and inequality, the politics of identity offers little vision of social justice. While the politics of recognition has advanced, the politics of redistribution has been in retreat. She advocates instead a 'bivalent' approach to social oppression that integrates the 'social and the cultural, the economic and the discursive' (p. 5). Their separation is flawed in both theory and practice: their simultaneous pursuit does not diminish the radical potential of disability politics. Indeed, the acceptance of cultural differences presumes some foundation of social equality.

Nancy Fraser argues instead for a 'transformative' political project that is allied to 'deconstruction'. This rejects the notion that differences are expressions of human diversity and are not to be set within a hierarchy, because it implies that 'anything goes' and that there is no basis for making normative judgements about whether some difference is acceptable or not, better or worse. The goal of those advocating a disability politics should be to break down the disabled/non-disabled polarity in a way that promotes redistribution in the political economic spheres while also deconstructing disabling cultural-valuational claims around 'able-bodied normality'.

While for supporters of 'identity politics' the emphasis on 'difference' is the first stage in any cultural revaluation, for critics it is more likely to sustain rather than undermine existing differences. Various strategies have been advanced as ways of achieving collective political action within an acceptance of (some) difference. 'Identities may be supplanted by issues, as substantive campaigns around housing, health, welfare, education, employment, immigration, reproduction and media representations combat the multidimensional oppression matrix' (Humphrey 1999: 175). Nevertheless, a politics of difference has yet to demonstrate its capacity to sustain a coherent and effective political programme. As Marta Russell (1998) argues, the challenge for disability politics is to 'build upon mutual respect and support *without dismissing or diluting difference*. For instance, to *move beyond ramps, we must first agree that ramps are indisputably necessary*. That would be making a common political "home", blending difference into commonality' (Russell 1998: 233).

Review

The remarkable politicization and mobilization of disabled people around the world has been extraordinarily significant in challenging myths about their 'inherent' passivity. The emergence of an organized and cohesive disabled people's movement has provided a political voice for disabled people. It has also had a significant influence on politicians, policy makers, and the population at large. At the national level, the most impressive demonstration of disabled people's self-organization are legislative innovations such as the 1990 Americans with Disabilities Act and similar anti-discrimination measures introduced in other parts of the world. Although these fall far short of the original objectives, they do represent significant advances in placing disability on the political agenda.

Another dimension to disability politics has been its involvement in less conventional forms. For some commentators it constitutes a 'new social movement' that rejects traditional pressure group and political party activities in favour of more radical aims and forms of struggle. Of more concern, from our perspective, is that disability politics has been caught up in the wider flow of identity politics and the celebration of difference. This has rightly focused concerns on cultural domination and the importance of attending to differences among disabled people, but tends to have lost sight of the goal of political-economic redistribution.

This is an appropriate point at which to turn the spotlight away from wealthier, industrialized countries, to consider disability issues in non-Western countries, with often very different and diverse social, economic, political and cultural experiences and contexts.

7

Disability and Development: Global Perspectives

Thus far we have focused on changing perceptions of impairment and disability in predominantly Western societies. Attention has centred on the growing challenge posed by social model analyses to conventional medical and lay orthodoxies in exploring the various economic, political and cultural barriers to mainstream society encountered by people with accredited impairments.

In this concluding chapter, we address selected disability issues in what is commonly referred to as the 'developing', 'third' or 'majority' world: namely, most of the 'poorer' countries outside Europe, North America, Australia and New Zealand. Disability has become a particular focus of attention in recent decades with the rise in political activism by disabled people and their organizations at the international level and increasing debate about the development of 'alternative' service programmes, most notably those adhering to community-based rehabilitation (CBR). We offer a critical examination of the politics and production of impairment and disability in majority world countries, and argue that disability is a complex, dynamic phenomenon that is increasingly influenced by the escalating processes of 'globalization', or the growing economic and social interdependence of nation-states.

Impairment in the majority world

Early advocates of the social model defined impairment as a biomedical issue, and concentrated instead on disability, as a social, economic, political and cultural phenomenon. Some commentators have responded that impairment is integral to the experience of disability, and therefore must not be omitted from social analyses of disability. However, any attempt to extend these debates beyond English-speaking countries to the majority world is confronted by an immediate dilemma: namely, that the key concepts defy easy translation into other languages and cultures. Thus, approaching impairment in biomedical and individualistic terms is peculiar to Western philosophical and cultural traditions (Miles 1995).

Considerable anthropological effort has been invested in exploring cross-cultural approaches that include the identification of people with impairments – from Emile Durkheim to Mary Douglas and Claude Lévi-Strauss (Ingstad and Whyte 1995). This literature demonstrates how ways of perceiving the individual, including the biological constitution of the body and concepts of health and ability, differ markedly across the diverse cultural systems of the majority world. As an illustration, the separation of body and mind became a characteristic feature of Enlightenment thinking in Euro-American societies, but outside these societies a very different perspective often prevails. For instance, in Chinese cultures, the mind, heart and body are treated as indistinguishable from each other. Consequently, it makes sense only to talk of the 'body-mind' as a single entity, in contrast to Western bio-medicine. Moreover, traditional Chinese medicine, which is still widely practised, constructs the body-mind as part of a wider constellation that includes lineage, family, community, country, nature and cosmos. From this perspective, illnesses and impairments are conceived as signs or products of imbalances in one of these constituent realms of the total body-mind system or between realms. This has important and specific implications for the ways in which people with impairments are perceived and treated by family and community members within Chinese society (Stone 1999b).

Studies looking at a wide range of countries document the very different ways in which different cultures perceive impairments and body-mind variations (Hanks and Hanks 1948; Scheer and Groce 1988; Miles 1992, 1995; Ingstad and Whyte 1995). This literature provides ample evidence of the considerable diversity in what is understood as impairment. Although most cultures have notions of a 'normal' or 'ideal' body-mind, and what constitute acceptable individual attributes, the specific character of those norms and the extent to which they are negotiable varies considerably across and within societies. Hence, what counts as an 'impairment' and what is regarded as an appropriate social response are far from universal features: 'The disfiguring scar in Dallas becomes an honorific mark in Dahomey' (Hanks and Hanks 1948: 11). Moreover, the assumed 'defects' that mark individuals out as unacceptably different may include features that other cultures regard as benign, such as freckles, small or flabby buttocks, and protruding navels (Ingstad and Whyte 1995: 6).

It is widely argued that religious ideas and teachings are the main determinant of what is socially acceptable in non-Western contexts, which means that the role of material factors in the creation of disability is largely overlooked. Even so, there is no consensus among major religions such as Hinduism, Islam and Buddhism about the 'correct' way to regard impairment, just as the impact of religious meanings on everyday thinking and practice is contested. Yet in societies where these religions claim wide popular allegiance, perceived impairments are significant for people's life chances, because they are widely regarded as 'misfortunes, sent by deity, fate, karma; often associated with parental sin' (Miles 1995: 52). These religions, like Christianity, also tend to emphasize ways of understanding and responding to misfortune through individual acceptance as a means of spiritual salvation (Charlton 1998). However, most social research in poorer countries has concentrated on responses to impairment in small-scale, rural-based groups, where religious beliefs may exert a stronger impact than they do on those living in urban environments (Scheer and Groce 1988; Ingstad and Whyte 1995).

In order to grasp the meaning and significance of impairment, how and why individuals are considered 'abnormal' or 'incompetent', and how control is exercised and resistance becomes manifest, it is illuminating to explore these issues within different cultural contexts. Ida Nicolaisen (1995) identifies 'humanity' and 'personhood' as key concepts. There is ample evidence that perceptions of *humanity* diverge significantly across non-capitalist societies. Cultures ranging from the ancient Greco-Roman to contemporary South Asian have constructed elaborate hierarchies to locate individuals along a continuum ranging from humanity to non-humanity. She further illustrates how in the case of the Punan Bah of Central Borneo, for example, only a narrow set of impairments, including epilepsy, 'madness' and severe birth defects, are regarded as evidence of not being human.

Furthermore, according to Mary Douglas (1966), responses to perceived physical, sensory or cognitive difference involve deep-seated psychological fears of 'anomaly'. This refers to the link between perceptions of impairment and a non-human status symptomatic of the 'Other' (that cannot be explained). Cultures deal with perceived ambiguity by either attempting to control it in some way or by adopting it as ritual. Examples include the Nuer practice of treating 'monstrous births as baby hippopotamuses, accidentally born to humans'. They respond by returning them to 'the river where they belong' (Douglas 1966: 39). Nancy Scheper-Hughes adds further examples of 'crocodile infants', 'poor little critters' in Northeast Brazil, and Irish 'changelings', and concludes that 'The sickly, wasted, or congenitally deformed infant challenges the tentative and fragile symbolic boundaries between human and non-human, natural and supernatural, normal and abominable' (Scheper-Hughes 1992: 375).

While infanticide directed at children with impairments is by no means a universal feature of 'traditional' societies, there are reports from both Asian and African societies that it is widely practised (Charlton 1998). For poor families and individuals who cannot afford enough food to eat, the presence of a young child or adult with an impairment can have devastating effects. A combination of desperate economic circumstances, lack of other support, cultural considerations and/or ignorance can result in families 'hiding' or abandoning their disabled offspring (Ingstad 2001).

Personhood signifies a refinement of the notion of humanity that differentiates between specific roles or statuses. It focuses on expectations of what it means to be a child, adult, man or woman, and therefore may change over the life course. Whereas in most Western societies personhood is equated with earning an income from work, in China it has been more associated with marriage and producing a son to continue the family lineage (Stone 1999b). However, perceived impairment does not necessarily lead to social exclusion. For example, among the Masai people of Kenya, people with physical impairments may marry, become parents and participate in all communal activities 'to the best of their abilities' (Talle 1995: 69).

What such examples indicate is the diversity of cultural responses to people with impairments in pre-capitalist and 'developing' societies. The range of participation of people with physical impairments stretches from nil in the case of the *pariah*, because the individual is deemed an economic or moral liability or threat, to *limited participation*, where the individual is granted selected social or other concessions, to *laissez-faire*, where some people enjoy opportunities to acquire prestige and wealth (Hanks and Hanks 1948; Ingstad and Whyte 1995).

Impairment: patterns and social origins

Most people in Western societies, and particularly professionals, presume that biomedical perceptions of normality are universal concepts, or ought to be. They ignore or dismiss other cultural perceptions of impairment, causation and local or family responses. Certainly, these beliefs informed the World Health Organization's *International Classification of Impairments, Disabilities and Handicaps* (WHO 1980). Cross-national data on the prevalence of 'impairments' and 'disabilities' must be treated with additional caution, because the collection and processing procedures vary significantly, with some countries relying on professional diagnoses and others on lay responses to questionnaires (United Nations 1990). If these concerns are set aside, the resulting league tables demonstrate that the prevalence of impairment amongst the world's population is lower than that of 'disability' or functional limitations: 'Among the 55 nations impairment rates varied between 0.2 per cent to around 6 per cent, whilst disability rates varied from approximately 7 per cent to 20.9 per cent' (Ingstad 2001: 773).

While these surveys suggest that most of the world's disabled population lives in the poorer nations of the majority world, the incidence of both reported impairment and 'disability' is generally higher in wealthier nations (United Nations 1990). There are several possible reasons for this. First, the wealthy countries of the minority world have better health and support services; hence, there is a greater survival rate among people born with impairments and amongst those who acquire them later in life. Second, the higher life expectancy, and hence larger proportion of people over fifty years old, in developed societies is linked directly with higher overall rates of impairment. Third, there are some conditions, such as dyslexia, that are regarded as 'disabling' in minority world countries but which present few problems to someone living in a rural village in Zimbabwe, and are therefore not perceived or reported as 'functional limitations' (Coleridge 1993).

The United Nations (1990) data also indicate that there is an urban bias towards perceived impairment within all societies. This is because urban areas generally have more medical 'rehabilitation' and support services, as well as greater risk of injury through pollution, traffic and work accidents, and perhaps more possibilities for earning a living by begging if one exposes one's impairments.

There are other noteworthy contrasts within and between countries. In some villages in Zaire, for example, more than 30 per cent of the community are effected by river blindness. In South Africa, as in many other societies, 'race' and ethnic factors exert a further significant impact, as is demonstrated in the marked differences in the geographical distribution and quality of medical services between 'race' groups. This means that a spinally injured person is ten times more likely to survive into late middle age if a white rather than a black person (Coleridge 1993).

The main causes of 'chronic diseases and long term impairments' in majority world countries are poverty, inadequate sanitation, poor diet and bad housing (WHO 2001). Furthermore, the disparity in wealth between the developed and developing world has widened steadily over the twentieth century and is now the largest it has ever been. It has been estimated that in 1820 the gap between the world's richest and poorest nation was approximately three to one. By 1992 it had risen to a staggering seventy-two to one (Giddens 2001: 70). It is little surprise that this has resulted in dire consequences for people living in the majority world. For example, more than 100 million people in these countries have acquired impairments because of chronic malnutrition. Every year 250,000 children lose their sight through a lack of vitamin A, which is usually provided by the regular intake of green vegetables. Perhaps as many as 800 million people are at risk of intellectual impairment due to a lack of iodine in their diet (Stone 1999a: 5).

These figures suggest that up to one-half of the world's impairment is preventable by the introduction of improved policies to confront poverty and malnutrition, to improve sanitation, drinking water and employment conditions, and to reduce accidents (Charlton 1998). From the perspective of those in a majority world, preventive measures are a top priority – hence the large and rising demand for basic public health and medical services. In some poorer countries, it has been calculated that 90 per cent of children with impairments die before they reach twenty years old, and the same percentage with 'mental impairments' do not live beyond their fifth birthday (UNESCO 1995: 9–14). There were more than 100,000 new cases of polio in majority world countries in 1994 (Stone 1999a: 5). In India, the prevalence of conditions such as polio and blindness is at least four times higher among people who are below the poverty line compared with those who are above it (Ghia 2001: 29).

Quite simply, a great deal of impairment is the direct outcome of skewed and exploitative economic and social development. The lack of funding to organize and deliver appropriate medical and 'disability related services' is exacerbated by the funding policies of international financial institutions such as the World Bank and the International Monetary Fund, which force national governments to cut back on public services to service enormous international debts. In practice, access to medical and allied services and treatments depends heavily on the ability to pay. This poses major problems for disabled people. Furthermore, the lack of trained medical personnel is exacerbated by the active recruitment of qualified staff from poor countries by richer nations. The loss is made worse because there is no financial compensation for countries to cover the cost of retraining new staff. This must be seen against a background where only 1 per cent of disabled people in the majority world has access to any form of 'rehabilitation' or disability-related services (WHO 2001).

In stark contrast, the idea of prevention has become a contested issue among disabled people's groups in wealthy developed societies because it is often juxtaposed with eugenics, euthanasia, selective abortion and attempts to deny the humanity of disabled people (see chapter 3). Moreover, in the minority world, a disproportionate amount of resources, both financial and human, are channelled into expensive medical innovations that 'will benefit only a relative minority of the world's population' (WHO 2001: 15). The wealthier nations of the world have witnessed considerable investment in cosmetic surgery and allied medical treatments to 'improve' an individual's appearance.

Of course, poverty and the lack of an adequate health and social care infrastructure are not the only factors producing impairment in the majority world. A fuller set of 'causes' of impairment extends to specific cultural practices (such as female genital mutilation), natural disasters (earthquakes, floods), and the consequences of economic development (industrial accidents and pollution) (*New Internationalist* 1992). Civil wars, often fanned by the international arms trade, have caused an unprecedented growth in civilians and military personnel with impairments. In Cambodia, an estimated 100,000 people lost limbs as a direct result of the combatants' use of landmines (UNESCO 1995). There was a similar growth in the number of people with impairments as a result of the recent violence in Rwanda. In such conflicts, a strategy of maiming rather than killing people was sometimes followed on the grounds that 'disabled people remain far more visible than the dead' (Coleridge 1993: 107), thus diminishing an opponent's economic and psychological assets and resistance.

The conclusion is, however, quite clear-cut: 'as far as the majority of the world's disabled people are concerned, impairment is very clearly, primarily the consequence of social and political factors, not an unavoidable "fact of nature"' (Abberley 1987: 11).

Disability and globalization

As outlined above, in order to understand the process of development, it must be set within a global context. Over the last few decades there has been a significant intensification of the processes of globalization. This encompasses the interconnectedness of individuals, groups and communities within worldwide economic, political and cultural networks, particularly as a result of the rapid development of information and communication technologies. It has resulted in some of the world's leading transnational corporations, such as Coca-Cola, General Motors and Exxon, becoming richer than a lot of majority world countries. Overall, globalization has greatly accelerated the imposition of a capitalist world order (Held et al. 1999).

Furthermore, the notion of 'development' is generally associated with Western economic, technological and cultural institutions and innovation, and is invariably perceived and presented in positive terms. From a majority world perspective, development is almost always equated with overall social progress and as something to which all countries should aspire. Yet terms such as 'developed' and 'developing' obscure the vast inequalities of wealth and resources that exist between 'richer' and 'poorer' nations. They also conceal the extent to which the minority world is actively engaged in the 'underdevelopment' of majority world countries by exercising its wide-ranging economic and political power (Charlton 1998). But there is also often an equally significant economic divide within many 'developing' nations.

More specifically for our analysis, the social origins of impairment and disability bear the clear imprint of Western-style economic, technological and cultural development. Although there may be significant differences in emphasis, there is general agreement that industrialization, urbanization, liberal utilitarianism and medicalization, along with cultural understandings of 'able-bodied normalcy', particularly as disseminated through Western media, have influenced the social construction of disability. This led to the systematic exclusion of disabled people from the mainstream of everyday life. These forces are now being exported more quickly than ever throughout the world. The end result is that the disabling tendencies generally associated with minority world economic and cultural development are being replicated throughout the majority world.

Ida Nicolaisen's (1995) analysis of the impact of Western capitalist social relations following the coming of logging companies to the Punan Bah economy and culture of Central Borneo illustrates the point well. Increased reliance on wage labour seriously undermined the status and role of particular individuals within the family group. As a result, collective responsibility for those viewed as economically 'dependent' – namely, people with impairments and older people no longer able to work – has been seriously undermined. Moreover, the large extended households that once facilitated the integration of such individuals into communal life are now breaking up into smaller, Western-style units with decreased capacity to provide support for the needs of individual members with an impairment. Meanwhile, expectations and attitudes to traditional belief systems are changing, so as to be more in line with 'capitalist Western values', and in so doing, 'imperceptibly permeate the Punan Bah view of themselves and the world' (Nicolaisen 1995: 54). In a similar fashion, the exposure of Masai society to market forces has undermined traditional support networks for people with impairments (Talle 1995), while studies of Southern Africa report that mothers of disabled children and disabled women are particularly vulnerable (S. Miles 1996).

Experiencing social exclusion

People with accredited impairments living in majority world countries experience much higher levels of poverty combined with more limited welfare systems and supports (Coleridge

1993; Charlton 1998). The causes of such disadvantages are not simply disabling attitudes and prejudices. They are deeply rooted in structural inequalities and social processes. For example, almost a third of the world's 'absolute poor' live in India. This level of poverty applies where people do not have enough resources to support a minimum of health and efficiency. Furthermore, 'while 48 per cent of India's people survive in absolute poverty . . . about two thirds are "capability poor" i.e. they do not receive the minimum level of education and health care, necessary for functioning human capabilities' (Sharif 1999, quoted by Ghia 2001: 28).

The marginalization and powerlessness experienced by disabled people living in isolated rural areas and urban slums across Africa, Asia and Latin America are too often overlooked. They are disproportionately unemployed, underemployed and underpaid. Moreover, few majority world countries have the resources to sustain anything like an adequate welfare safety net for those worst off. Between 65 and 80 per cent of India's estimated 60 million disabled people live in areas where public amenities such as clean water, electricity and sanitation are often non-existent. When juxtaposed with the lack of the most basic medical treatments and support systems, 'the problems of inequality and injustice are so massive as to appear unmanageable' (Ghia 2001: 29). In the same vein, a Brazilian disabled activist argues that disabled people are reduced to living in a 'pitiful condition', as 'outcasts deprived of social life, dignity, and citizenship' (Rosangela Bieler, quoted by Charlton 1998: 19).

Women and children with impairments experience particularly high levels of poverty, leading to chronic malnutrition and difficulty in resisting debilitating sickness.

> Women in many parts of India are routinely fed last and least. Not only is there overwhelming evidence of differential food intake, but there is also evidence that girls are given poorer quality medical care. . . . girls are admitted to hospital less often than boys are, and when admitted are often in a dangerous condition. (Ghia 2001: 30)

Education is frequently presented as a means of addressing the problem of poverty and as a means to social inclusion (although many disabled people in minority world countries might dispute its effectiveness). However, in some majority world countries disabled children, most particularly girls, are denied any formal schooling whatsoever (UNESCO 1995). Furthermore, the transfer of the types of schooling and skills favoured in Western societies may prove more exclusionary or less relevant to majority world needs (Kalyanpur 1996; S. Miles 1996). In particular, the Westernized school system promotes a particular notion of the skills necessary to achieve social and economic competence. This has led to the labelling of some children as 'educationally backward', or having 'learning difficulties'. This results in their marginalization, even from contexts where numeracy and literacy skills may not be vital to an individual's life chances (Ingstad 2001).

Disabled people must also confront considerable shortfalls in appropriate support systems, ranging from a lack of personal assistance schemes to under-resourced organizations charged with their support. In addition, there is a serious shortage of equipment, aids and accessible technology, such as brailling machines and computers, wheelchairs and prostheses. A specific issue for people with hearing impairments is the serious shortage of sign language interpreters in many countries. Often where basic support items are available, disabled individuals cannot afford to buy them, while alternatives – for example, to assist mobility – are often inadequate and sometimes degrading (Charlton 1998).

These support problems are complemented by inaccessible transport systems and built environments. Moreover, there is little short-term prospect of moving significantly towards satisfying accessible housing or transport needs when overall standards are low. Environmental access is again a major concern in the densely populated and rapidly expanding cities of the majority world. For example, one commentator reports that:

> In all my travels, Bangkok, where 40 percent of the Thai people live, is the hardest city to get around. Although the actual structural inaccessibility (lack of ramps, curb cuts, elevators) is more or less the same throughout the Third World, the streets of Bangkok are almost impossible to cross

... Bangkok is a wheelchair user's nightmare. Jakarta and Bombay are close runners-up. (Charlton 1998: 106)

As in the minority world, the experience of social exclusion over recent decades has been accompanied by a growing politicization of disabled people. International contacts in the 1980s had a particularly galvanizing effect for many disabled activists and disability rights organizations. The conflicts between old and new disability politics emerged at the meeting of Rehabilitation International in 1980 in Singapore. Dissident disabled representatives left to set up what became the Disabled Peoples' International. As Joshua Malinga from Zimbabwe commented: 'When I went to Singapore I was a conservative, but when I returned I was very radical' (quoted in Charlton 1998: 133).

A growing interest internationally in disability can be traced back to the 1970s, with the United Nations' *Declaration on the Rights of Mentally Retarded Persons* (1971), followed shortly after by the *Declaration of the Rights of Disabled Persons* (1975). Furthermore, 1981 was designated the International Year of Disabled Persons and 1983–92 the Decade for Disabled Persons. The apparent radical thrust of these initiatives cannot obscure their foundation on conventional individualistic, medical notions of disability and rehabilitation. For example, a primary aim of the International Year of Disabled Persons was to 'help disabled people in their physical and psychological adjustment to society'.

Over the last three decades there has been a succession of initiatives promoting a programme of disability rights (Sayce 2000). One important example is the *Standard Rules on the Equalization of Opportunities for Persons with Disabilities* (United Nations 1993). This comprises twenty-two standard rules to facilitate full participation and equality for 'persons with disabilities'. These cover aspects of daily living, including awareness raising, medical and support services, education, employment, leisure and cultural activities. However, its stated intentions have not been matched by the required action. Rhetoric in international organizations often outruns policy implementation at national levels, particularly as majority world governments have very limited resources to bring about radical changes in the lives of disabled people.

Community-based rehabilitation

One area where there has been considerable activity with financial and other support from minority world countries for developing accessible services has been in community-based rehabilitation (CBR) projects and programmes. The concept of CBR was conceived and championed by WHO with the aim of making 'disability and rehabilitation' services available to grass-roots communities in a cost-effective way. The thinking behind CBR has subsequently been adapted, contested and reworked in a widening range of settings. There are now cadres of Western or Western-trained professionals (planners, implementers, evaluators and specialist rehabilitation staff) working on disability-related issues in majority world CBR programmes supported by international funding, networks, training manuals and programmes, conferences and journals (Stone 1999a).

For critics, early CBR projects represented updated but ill-disguised versions of what colonizing countries have been attempting to do over the last two centuries. Medical and related services, along with education, were often organized and provided by missionaries and associated charities from the colonial power. The idea was that disadvantaged and dependent groups such as disabled and other poor people should be supported by charitable fund-raising and private donations. In some countries, this coincided with traditions of almsgiving in religions such as Islam and Hinduism. Such ideas have continued to characterize and envelop services for disabled people in developing nations to this day, and may help explain (aside from their lack of finance) why so many governments within the majority world are reluctant 'to commit to full responsibility for disabled citizens' (Ingstad 2001: 778).

Given such a legacy, many CBR projects have been rightly criticized for, at best, being well-meaning but ill-conceived and, at worst, ideologically and culturally biased with a concealed political agenda. One frequent response to CBR initiatives has been criticism for their lack of sensitivity to local cultures and practices. Moreover, they have not produced the promised tangible and long-term impact on the lives of disabled people, their families, or local communities as a whole (Stone 1999a; WHO 2001). This has raised fundamental questions about whether CBR programmes have been planned and implemented before local communities have had an opportunity to express their own needs and priorities (Thomas and Thomas 2002).

More recently, however, there have been some important changes in the organization of CBR. This is associated with the changing role of international non-government organizations (NGOs) and the increasing priority placed on the involvement of disabled people at all levels and in all contexts by important sponsors of CBR programmes. Whereas NGOs involved in rehabilitation used to be dependent almost exclusively on their own resources for funding, today they increasingly rely on external funding. A number of governments, such as those of Norway and Sweden, have been particularly prominent donors. Despite obvious concerns about the continuity of funding and whether any strings are attached, their involvement has helped to shift the CBR emphasis from largely short-term, small-scale operations driven by a predominantly medical model of disability to larger, long-term strategies. The CBR philosophy has also become oriented more towards 'community development and the promotion of equal rights' (Ingstad 2001: 786). Most importantly, there is growing recognition that disabled people, their families and key representatives of local communities must be meaningfully involved at every level and at every stage in the planning and implementation of CBR projects and strategies. Nevertheless, the possibility remains that the larger community will not necessarily accede to the expressed priorities and support needs of a (disabled) minority. An associated issue is whether disabled people should have separate programmes or be integrated into the wider community rehabilitation process (WHO 2001).

There must be doubts about the accuracy of predictions that CBR was a relatively less expensive option. Some of the saving was achievable only by giving families of disabled people a much higher profile in rehabilitation services and interventions. In practice, this often added considerable extra responsibilities, as well as creating extraordinarily difficult dilemmas for families with a disabled member in deciding how to allocate their (programme) time and resources. In some instances it meant that individuals with multiple impairments lost out because their support needs were so much greater than those of singly impaired people. In some cultures, disabled women are disadvantaged relative to disabled men in the allocation of services. This is attributed to their established exclusion from full participation in community life, or else it is a result of the domination of rehabilitation services by male service providers. The shortage of female rehabilitation staff has been a further barrier to involving disabled women in CBR programmes in some cultures (Thomas and Thomas 2002).

A key stimulus in radicalizing the involvement of NGOs has been the increasingly high profile accorded disabled people and their organizations in national and international politics. As discussed in chapter 6, over the past two decades there has been a dramatic increase in organizations controlled and run by disabled people. Local, national and international organizations have taken a more prominent and assertive role in promoting social change based on their own sociopolitical interpretations of disability. The continuing growth of organizations of disabled people has been crucial in generating political campaigns and raising awareness of disability issues, across many majority world nations (Jayasooria and Ooi 1994). The establishment of international networks and newsletters has had an additional facilitative role in helping to sustain this process. Examples include the activities of Disabled Peoples' International, the international umbrella for national organizations controlled and run by disabled people, and Disability Awareness in Action, a project led by disabled people to promote increased networking amongst disabled people and their organizations worldwide.

Review

There is a small but growing body of reports and publications that explore disability in the majority world. For the most part these are practitioner-led and practice-based. The focus is on practical interventions: disability support services, education and income generation. In most cases these publications offer useful evaluations of processes and outcomes, but rarely do they deal with the exploration of wider issues, such as belief systems, cultural responses and attitudes, life chances, local policies and practices and aspirations. By way of contrast, there has been an expanding literature from writers within the disability and development field who have argued for a more critical approach to disability in a majority world context. These studies look beyond medical rehabilitation interventions to analyse local and cultural interpretations of impairment and disability within the rapidly changing world of the twenty-first century (Coleridge 1993; Ingstad and Whyte 1995; Stone 1999a).

The globalization of disability has been linked with a range of consequences, more often negative than positive. Where Western-trained activists, academics and practitioners are working with or for disabled people in majority world settings, crucial questions of risk must be raised. Whose agenda dominates? Whose definition of impairment and disability prevails? Whose ideology and culture determine policy and practice? On what criteria are outcomes measured? (Stone 1999a: 9). Most significantly, raising these questions, which are long overdue, has been crucial in signalling that both impairment and disability in the majority world are firmly on the academic and political agenda. This must be welcomed. So too must the small but growing cadre of disability activists, scholars and researchers whose work has helped deepen our understanding of the relationship between impairment, disability and development in majority world contexts. Overall, the politics of impairment is inseparable from the politics of global poverty and inequality, and the social, economic, political and cultural changes resulting from capitalist industrialization and globalization. It is particularly important given that these developments will almost certainly have profound implications for everyone, whether disabled or not, and regardless of whether they live in the minority or the majority world.

References

Abberley, P. 1987: The concept of oppression and the development of a social theory of disability. *Disability, Handicap and Society*, 2 (1), 5–19.

Abrams, P. 1968: *The Origins of British Sociology 1834–1914*. Chicago: University of Chicago Press.

Albrecht, G. L. (ed.) 1976: *The Sociology of Physical Disability and Rehabilitation*. Pittsburgh: University of Pittsburgh Press.

Albrecht, G. L. 1992: *The Disability Business*. London: Sage.

Anderson, E. M. and Clarke, L. 1982: *Disability in Adolescence*. London: Methuen.

Anderson, R. and Bury, M. (eds) 1988: *Living with Chronic Illness: The Experience of Patients and their Families*. London: Unwin Hyman.

Anspach, R. 1979: From stigma to identity politics: political activism among the physically disabled and former mental patients. *Social Science and Medicine*, 13A, 765–73.

Armstrong, D. 1983: *Political Anatomy of the Body: Medical Knowledge in Britain in the Twentieth Century*. Cambridge: Cambridge University Press.

Armstrong, F. and Barton, L. (eds) 1999: *Disability, Human Rights and Education*. Buckingham: Open University Press.

Asch, A. and Fine, M. 1988: Introduction: beyond pedestals. In M. Fine and A. Asch (eds), *Women with Disabilities: Essays in Psychology, Culture, and Politics*, Philadelphia: Temple University Press, 1–37.

Bagilhole, B. 1997: *Equal Opportunities and Social Policy*. London: Longman.

Bank-Mikkelson, N. 1980: Denmark. In R. J. Flynn and K. E. Nitsch (eds), *Normalisation, Social Integration and Community Services*, Baltimore: University Park Press, 51–70.

Barnes, C. 1990: *Cabbage Syndrome: The Social Construction of Dependence*. London: Falmer.

Barnes, C. 1991: *Disabled People in Britain and Discrimination*. London: Hurst and Co., in association with the British Council of Organizations of Disabled People.

Barnes, C. 1992: *Disabling Imagery and the Media: An Exploration of Media Representations of Disabled People*. Belper, Derbyshire, The British Council of Organizations of Disabled People.

Barnes, C. 1997: A legacy of oppression: a history of disability in Western culture. In L. Barton and M. Oliver (eds), *Disability Studies: Past, Present and Future*, Leeds: Disability Press, 3–24.

Barnes, C. and Mercer, G. (eds) 1996a: *Exploring the Divide: Illness and Disability*. Leeds: Disability Press.

Barnes, C. and Mercer, G. 1996b: Introduction. In C. Barnes and G. Mercer (eds), *Exploring the Divide: Illness and Disability*, Leeds: Disability Press, 1–16.

Barnes, C. and Oliver, M. 1995: Disability rights: rhetoric and reality in the UK. *Disability and Society*, 10 (1), 111–16.

Barnes, C., Mercer, G. and Shakespeare, T. 1999: *Exploring Disability*. Cambridge: Polity.

Barnes, M. 1997: *Care, Communities and Citizens*. London: Longman.

Battye, L. 1966: The Chatterley syndrome. In P. Hunt, *Stigma*, London: Geoffrey Chapman, 2–16.

Bauman, Z. 1990: *Thinking Sociologically*. Oxford: Blackwell.

Baxter, C., Poonia, K., Ward, L. and Nadirshaw, Z. (1990) *Double Discrimination: Issues and Services for People with Learning Difficulties from Black and Ethnic Minority Communities*. London: King's Fund Centre.

Baynton, D. 1992: A silent exile on this earth: metaphorical construction of deafness in the nineteenth century. *American Quarterly*, 44 (2), 216–43.

Beck, U. 1992: *Risk Society: Towards a New Modernity*. London: Sage.

Becker, H. 1963: *Outsiders: Studies in the Sociology of Deviance*. New York: Free Press.

Begum, N. 1992: Disabled women and the feminist agenda. *Feminist Review*, 40 (Spring), 70–84.

Begum, N. 1994: Mirror, mirror on the wall. In N. Begum, M. Hill and A. Stevens (eds), *Reflections: Views of Black Disabled People on their Lives and Community Care*, London: Central Council for Education and Training of Social Work, 17–36.

Begum, N., Hill, M. and Stevens, A. (eds) 1994: *Reflections: Views of Black Disabled People on their Lives and Community Care*, London: Central Council for the Education and Training of Social Work.

Beresford, P. 2000: What have madness and psychiatric system survivors got to do with disability and disability studies? *Disability and Society*, 15 (1), 167–72.

Berger, J. 1972: *Ways of Seeing*. London: British Broadcasting Corporation and Penguin.

Berkowitz, E. 1987: *Disabled Policy: America's Programs for the Handicapped*. Cambridge: Cambridge University Press.

Berthoud, R. et al. 1993: *The Economic Problems of Disabled People*. London: Policy Studies Institute.

Bickenbach, J. E. 1993: *Physical Disability and Social Policy*. Toronto: University of Toronto Press.

Bickenbach, J. E. 1999: Minority rights or universal participation: the politics of disablement. In M. Jones and L. A. B. Marks (eds), *Disability, Divers-ability and Legal Change*, The Hague: Kluwer Law International/Martinus Nijhoff Publishers, 101–15.

Biklen, D. and Bogdan, R. 1977: Media portrayals of disabled people: a study of stereotypes. *Interracial Books for Children Bulletin*, 8 (6 and 7), 4–7.

Blaxter, M. 1976: *The Meaning of Disability*. London: Heinemann.

Blaxter, M. 1984: Letter in response to Williams. *Social Science and Medicine*, 17 (15), 104.

Bogdan, R. 1996: The social construction of freaks. In R. G. Thomson (ed.), *Freakery: Culture Spectacles of the Extraordinary Body*, New York: New York University Press, 23–37.

Booth, T. and Booth, W. 1998: *Growing Up with Parents who have Learning Difficulties*. London: Routledge.

Bourdieu, P. 1973: Cultural reproduction and social reproduction. In R. Brown (ed.), *Knowledge, Education, and Cultural Change*, London: Tavistock, 71–112.

Bowe, F. 1978: *Handicapping America*. New York: Harper and Row.

Brah, A. 1992: Difference, diversity and differentiation. In J. Donald and A. Rattansi (eds), *'Race', Culture and Difference*, London: Sage, 126–45.

Brattgard, S. O. 1974: Social and psychological aspects of the situation of the disabled. In D. M. Boswell and J. M. Wingrove (eds), *The Handicapped Person in the Community*, London: Tavistock Publications and the Open University Press, 7–9.

Bredberg, E. 1999: Writing disability history: problems, perspectives and sources. *Disability and Society*, 14 (2), 189–201.

Bristo, M. 2000: Letter of transmittal. In National Council on

Disability, *Promises to Keep: A Decade of Federal Enforcement of the Americans with Disabilities Act*, Washington, DC: National Council on Disability, 1.

Brittan, A. and Maynard, M. 1984: *Sexism, Racism and Oppression*. Oxford: Blackwell.

Brown, H. and Smith, H. (eds) 1992: *Normalisation: A Reader for the Nineties*. London: Tavistock.

Brown, S. E. 1997: 'Oh, don't you envy us our privileged lives?': a review of the disability culture movement. *Disability and Rehabilitation*, 19 (8), 339–49.

Brown, S. E., Connors, D. and Stern, N. (eds) 1985: *With the Power of Each Breath: A Disabled Women's Anthology*. Pittsburgh: Cleis Press.

Burchardt, T. 2000a: The dynamics of being disabled. *Journal of Social Policy*, 29 (4), 645–68.

Burchardt, T. 2000b: *Enduring Economic Exclusion: Disabled People, Income and Work*. York: Joseph Rowntree Foundation.

Burleigh, M. 1994: *Death and Deliverance: 'Euthanasia' in Germany 1900–1945*. Cambridge: Cambridge University Press.

Burr, V. 1995: *An Introduction to Social Constructionism*. London: Routledge.

Bury, M. 1996: Defining and researching disability: challenges and responses. In C. Barnes and G. Mercer (eds), *Exploring the Divide: Illness and Disability*, Leeds: Disability Press, 17–38.

Bury, M. 1997: *Health and Illness in a Changing Society*. London: Routledge.

Busfield, J. 1986: *Managing Madness*. London: Hutchinson.

Campbell, J. and Oliver, M. 1996: *Disability Politics: Understanding our Past, Changing our Future*. London: Routledge.

Campling, J. (ed.) 1979: *Better Lives for Disabled Women*. London: Virago.

Campling, J. (ed.) 1981: *Images of Ourselves: Women with Disabilities Talking*. London: Routledge and Kegan Paul.

Castel, R. 1983: Moral treatment: mental therapy and social control in the nineteenth century. In S. Cohen and A. Scull (eds), *Social Control and the State*, Oxford: Blackwell, 248–66.

Castells, M. 1996: *The Information Age: Economy, Society and Culture*, vol. 1: – *The Rise of the Network Society*. Malden, MA: Blackwell Publishers.

Cawson, A. 1982: *Corporatism and Welfare: Social Policy and State Intervention in Britain*. London: Heinemann.

Centre for Independent Living 1982: Independent living: the right to choose. In M. Eisenberg et al. (eds), *Disabled People as Second-Class Citizens*, New York: Springer Publishing Company, 250–63.

Chappell, A. L. 1992: Towards a sociological critique of the normalisation principle. *Disability, Handicap and Society*, 7 (1), 35–51.

Chappell, A. L. 1997: From normalisation to where? In L. Barton and M. Oliver (eds), *Disability Studies: Past, Present and Future*, Leeds: Disability Press, 45–61.

Chappell, A. L. 1998: Still out in the cold: people with learning difficulties and the social model of disability. In T. Shakespeare (ed.), *The Disability Reader: Social Science Perspectives*, London: Cassell, 211–20.

Charlton, J. I. 1998: *Nothing About Us Without Us: Disability Oppression and Empowerment*. Berkeley: University of California Press.

Charmaz, K. 1983: Loss of self: a fundamental form of suffering in the chronically ill. *Sociology of Health and Illness*, 5, 168–95.

Charmaz, K. 1987: Struggling for self: identity levels of the chronically ill. In J. A. Roth and P. Conrad (eds), *Research in the Sociology of Health Care*, vol. 6: *The Experience and Management of Chronic Illness*, Greenwich, CT: JAI Press, 283–321.

Chenoweth, L. 1999: Sexual abuse of people with disabilities: denied sexuality and abuses of power. In M. Jones and L. A. B. Marks (eds), *Disability, Divers-ability and Legal Change*. The Hague: Kluwer Law International/Martinus Nijhoff Publishers, 301–12.

Chouinard, V. 1997: Making space for disabling differences: challenging ableist geographies. *Environment and Planning D: Society and Space*, 15 (4), 379–87.

Christie, I. with Mensah-Coker, G. 1999: *An Inclusive Future? Disability, Social Change and Opportunities for Greater Inclusion by 2010*. London: Demos.

Clinard, M. B. and Meier, R. F. 1989: *Sociology of Deviant Behaviour*, 7th edn. Fort Worth, TX: Holt, Rinehart and Winston.

Cohen, S. and Scull, A. (eds) 1983: *Social Control and the State*. Oxford: Blackwell.

Cole, H. 1979: What's new about independent living? *Archives of Physical Medicine and Rehabilitation*, 60, 458–62.

Coleridge, P. 1993: *Disability, Liberation and Development*. Oxford: Oxfam Publications.

Confederation of Indian Organizations 1987: *Double Bind: To Be Disabled and Asian*. London: Confederation of Indian Organizations.

Conrad, P. and Schneider, J. W. 1980: *Deviance and Medicalization: From Badness to Sickness*. St Louis: Mosby.

Cooper, C. 1997: Can a fat woman call herself disabled? *Disability and Society*, 12 (1): 31–41.

Corbett, J. 1998: *Special Educational Needs in the Twentieth Century: A Cultural Analysis.* London: Cassell.

Corbett, J. and Ralph, S. 1994: Empowering adults: the changing imagery of charity advertising. *Australian Disability Review*, 1, 5–14.

Corbin, J. and Strauss, A. L. 1985: Managing chronic illness at home. *Qualitative Sociology*, 8, 224–47.

Corker, M. 1993: Integration and deaf people: the policy and power of enabling environments. In J. Swain, V. Finkelstein, S. French and M. Oliver (eds), *Disabling Barriers – Enabling Environments*, London: Sage, 145–54.

Corker, M. 1998a: *Deaf and Disabled, or Deafness Disabled?* Buckingham: Open University Press.

Corker, M. 1998b: Disability discourse in a postmodern world. In T. Shakespeare (ed.), *Disability Studies Reader*, London: Cassell, 221–33.

Corker, M. 1999: New disability discourse, the principle of optimization and social change. In M. Corker and S. French (eds), *Disability Discourse*, Buckingham: Open University Press, 192–209.

Corker, M. and French, S. 1999: Reclaiming discourse in disability studies. In M. Corker and S. French (eds), *Disability Discourse*, Buckingham: Open University Press, 1–11.

Cornes, P. 1991: Impairment, disability, handicap and new technology. In M. Oliver (ed.), *Social Work: Disabled People and Disabling Environments*, London: Jessica Kingsley, 98–114.

Crawford, R. C. 1980: Healthism and the medicalisation of everyday life. *International Journal of Health Services*, 10 (3), 365–88.

Croft, S. and Beresford, P. 1992: *Involving People in Social Services: From Paternalism to Participation.* London: Open Service Project/Joseph Rowntree Foundation.

Crow, L. 1996: Including all of our lives: renewing the social model of disability. In C. Barnes and G. Mercer (eds), *Exploring the Divide: Illness and Disability*, Leeds: Disability Press, 55–73.

CSO 2000: *Social Trends 30.* London: Central Statistics Office.

Cumberbatch, G. and Negrine, R. 1992: *Images of Disability on Television.* London: Routledge.

Daniel, C. 1998: Radical, angry and willing to work. *New Statesman*, 6 March, 22–3.

Darke, P. 1994: *The Elephant Man* (David Lynch, EMI Films, 1980): an analysis from a disabled perspective. *Disability and Society*, 9 (3), 327–42.

Darke, P. 1995: Autobiographies of discovery. *Disability Arts Magazine*, 5, 2 (Summer), 11–13.

Darke, P. 1998: Understanding cinematic representations of disability. In T. Shakespeare (ed.), *The Disability Studies Reader*, London: Cassell, 181–97.

Dartington, T., Miller, E. J. and Gwynne, G. 1981: *A Life Together*. London: Tavistock.

Darwin, C. 1922: *The Descent of Man and Selection in Relation to Sex*. New York: Appleton.

Davidson, F. W. K. et al. 1994: Images of disability in 19th century British children's literature, *Disability and Society*, 9 (1), 33–47.

Davis, A. 1989: *From Where I Sit: Living with Disability in an Able Bodied World*. London: Triangle.

Davis, F. 1961: Deviance disavowal: the management of strained interaction by the visibly handicapped. *Social Problems*, 9, 120–32.

Davis, K. and Mullender, A. 1993: *Ten Turbulent Years: A Review of the Work of the Derbyshire Coalition of Disabled People*. Nottingham: University of Nottingham Centre for Social Action.

Davis, L. J. 1995: *Enforcing Normalcy: Disability, Deafness, and the Body*. London and New York: Verso.

Davis, L. J. (ed.) 1997a: *The Disability Studies Reader*. London: Routledge.

Davis, L. J. 1997b: The need for Disability Studies. In L. J. Davis (ed.), *The Disability Studies Reader*, London: Routledge, 1–6.

Davis, L. J. 1999: Riding with the man on the escalator: citizenship and disability. In M. Jones and L. A. B. Marks (eds), *Disability, Divers-ability and Legal Change*. The Hague: Kluwer Law International/Martinus Nijhoff Publishers, 65–74.

Dear, M. J. and Wolch, J. R. 1987: *Landscapes of Despair: From Deinstitutionalisation to Homelessness*. Cambridge: Polity.

Deegan, M. J. and Brooks, N. (eds) 1985: *Women and Disability: The Double Handicap*. New Brunswick, NJ: Transaction Books.

DeJong, G. 1979: *The Movement for Independent Living: Origins, Ideology and Implications for Disability Research*. East Lansing: Michigan State University Press.

DeJong, G. 1983: Defining and implementing the Independent Living concept. In N. Crewe and I. Zola (eds), *Independent Living for Physically Disabled People*, London: Jossey-Bass, 239–48.

Dench, S., Meager, N. and Morris, S. 1996: *The Recruitment and Retention of People with Disabilities*. Brighton: Institute for Employment Studies.

DfEE 1997: *Excellence in Schools*. London: Department for Education and Employment, HMSO.

DfEE 1998: *Excellence for All: Meeting Special Educational Needs*. London: Department for Education and Employment, HMSO.

Disability Tribune 2000: Lives not worth living. London: Disability Awareness in Action, August, 1–2.

Douglas, M. 1966: *Purity and Danger*. London: Routledge and Kegan Paul.

Doyal, Len and Gough, I. 1991: *A Theory of Human Need*. Basingstoke: Macmillan.

Doyle, B. 1999: From welfare to rights? Disability and legal change in the United Kingdom in the late 1990s. In M. Jones and L. A. B. Marks (eds), *Disability, Divers-ability and Legal Change*. The Hague: Kluwer Law International/Martinus Nijhoff Publishers, 209–26.

DPI 1982: *Proceedings of the First World Congress*. Singapore: Disabled People's International.

Drake, R. 1996: A critique of the role of the traditional charities. In L. Barton (ed.), *Disability and Society: Emerging Issues and Insights*, London: Longman, 147–66.

Drake, R. 1999: *Understanding Disability Policies*. Basingstoke: Macmillan.

Driedger, D. 1989: *The Last Civil Rights Movement: Disabled People's International*. London: Hurst and Company.

Driedger, D. and Gray, S. (eds) 1992: *Imprinting Our Image: An International Anthology by Women with Disabilities*. Charlotte-town, Prince Edward Island: Gynergy Books.

Economist 1994: 13 August, 33–4.

Eisenberg, M. G., Griggins, C. and Duval, R. J. (eds) 1982: *Disabled People as Second-Class Citizens*. New York: Springer Publishing Company.

Eliot, T. S. 1968: *Christianity and Culture*. New York: Harvest/Harcourt Brace Jovanovich.

Enticott, J., Graham, P. and Lamb, B. 1992: *Polls Apart: Disabled People and the 1992 General Election*. London: Spastics Society.

European Commission 2001: *Disability and Social Participation in Europe*. Luxembourg: European Commission.

Fagan, T. and Lee, P. 1997: New social movements and social policy: a case study of the disability movement. In M. Lavalette and A. Pratt (eds), *Social Policy: A Conceptual and Theoretical Introduction*, London: Sage, 140–60.

Fawcett, B. 2000: *Feminist Perspectives on Disability*. London: Prentice-Hall.

Featherstone, M. 1991: The body in consumer culture. In M. Featherstone, M. Hepworth and B. S. Turner (eds), *The Body: Social Process and Cultural Theory*, London: Sage, 170–96.

Ferguson, P. M. 1994: *Abandoned to their Fate: Social Policy and Practices toward Severely Retarded People in America*. Philadelphia: Temple University Press.

Fine, M. and Asch, A. 1981: Disabled women: sexism without the pedestal. *Journal of Sociology and Social Welfare*, 8 (2), 233–48.

Fine, M. and Asch, A. 1988: *Women with Disabilities: Essays in Psychology, Culture, and Politics*. Philadelphia: Temple University Press.

Finger, A. 1991: *Past Due: A Story of Disability, Pregnancy and Birth*. London: Women's Press.

Finger, A. 1992: Forbidden fruit. *New Internationalist*, 233, 8–10.

Finkelstein, V. 1980: *Attitudes and Disabled People*. New York: World Rehabilitation Fund.

Finkelstein, V. 1983: Disability and the helper/helped relationship: an historical view. In A. Brechin, P. Liddiard and J. Swain (eds), *Handicap in a Social World*, Milton Keynes: Hodder and Stoughton in association with the Open University, 58–63.

Finkelstein, V. 1993a: The commonality of disability. In J. Swain, V. Finkelstein, S. French and M. Oliver (eds), *Disabling Barriers – Enabling Environments*, London: Sage in association with the Open University, 9–16.

Finkelstein, V. 1993b: Disability: a social challenge or an administrative responsibility? In J. Swain, V. Finkelstein, S. French and M. Oliver (eds), *Disabling Barriers – Enabling Environments*, London: Sage in association with the Open University, 34–43.

Finkelstein, V. 1996: Outside, "inside out". *Coalition*, April, 30–6.

Finkelstein V. and Stuart, O. 1996: Developing new services. In G. Hales (ed.), *Beyond Disability: Towards an Enabling Society*, London: Sage, 170–87.

Foucault, M. 1977: *Discipline and Punish*. London: Allen Lane.

Foucault, M. 1979: *The History of Sexuality*, vol. 1: *An Introduction*. London: Allen Lane.

Foucault, M. 1980: *Power/Knowledge*, ed. C. Gordon. Brighton: Harvester Press.

Foucault, M. 1982: The subject and power. In H. Dreyfus and P. Rabinow (eds), *Beyond Structuralism and Hermeneutics*, Brighton: Harvester Press, 208–26.

Fraser, N. 1995: From redistribution to recognition? Dilemmas of justice in a 'Post-Socialist' Age. *New Left Review*, 212, 68–73.

Fraser, N. 1997a: *Justice Interruptus: Critical Reflections on the 'Postsocialist' Condition*. New York and London: Routledge.

Fraser, N. 1997b: A rejoinder to Iris Young. *New Left Review*, 223 (May/June), 126–30.

Freidson, E. 1965: Disability as social deviance. In M. B. Sussman (ed.), *Sociology and Rehabilitation*, Washington, DC: American Sociological Association, 71–99.

Freidson, E. 1970: *Profession of Medicine*. New York: Harper and Row.

French, S. 1993: Disability, impairment or something in between? In J. Swain, V. Finkelstein, S. French and M. Oliver (eds), *Disabling Barriers – Enabling Environments*, London: Sage in association with the Open University, 17–25.

Gallagher, C. and Laqueur, T. 1987: *The Making of the Modern Body*. Berkeley: University of California Press.

Garland, R. 1995: *The Eye of the Beholder: Deformity and Disability in the Graeco-Roman World*. London: Duckworth.

Gartner, A. and Joe, T. (eds) 1987: *Images of the Disabled, Disabling Images*. New York: Praeger.

Gerber, D. 1996: The careers of people exhibited in freak shows: the problem of volition and valorisation. In R. G. Thomson (ed.), *Freakery: Culture Spectacles of the Extraordinary Body*, New York: New York University Press, 38–53.

Ghia, A. 2001: Marginalization and disability: experiences from the Third World. In M. Priestley (ed.), *Disability and the Life Course*, Cambridge: Cambridge University Press, 26–37.

Giddens, A. 1981: *A Contemporary Critique of Historical Materialism*. London: Macmillan.

Giddens, A. 1982: *Sociology: A Brief but Critical Introduction*. London: Macmillan.

Giddens, A. 1990: *The Consequences of Modernity*. Cambridge: Polity.

Giddens, A. 1991: *Modernity and Self-Identity*. Cambridge: Polity.

Giddens, A. 2001: *Sociology*, 4th edn. Cambridge: Polity.

Gilderbloom, J. I. and Rosentraub, M. S. 1990: Creating the accessible city: proposals for providing housing and transportation for low income, elderly and disabled people. *American Journal of Economics and Sociology*, 49 (3), 271–82.

Gillespie-Sells, K. et al., 1998: *She Dances to Different Drums: Research into Disabled Women's Sexuality*. London: King's Fund.

Gillman, M., Swain, J. and Heyman. B. 1997: Life history or 'care history': the objectification of people with learning difficulties through the tyranny of professional discourses. *Disability and Society*, 12 (5), 675–94.

Gleeson, B. J. 1997: Disability Studies: a historical materialist view. *Disability and Society*, 12 (2), 179–202.

Gleeson, B. J. 1999: *Geographies of Disability*. London: Routledge.

Gliedman, J. and Roth, W. 1980: *The Unexpected Minority*. New York: Harcourt Brace Jovanovich.

Goffman, E. 1961: *Asylums: Essays on the Social Situation of Mental Patients and Other Inmates*. New York: Doubleday; Harmondsworth: Pelican, 1968.

Goffman, E. 1963: *Stigma: Some Notes on the Management of*

Spoiled   Identity. Englewood   Cliffs,   NJ: Prentice-Hall; Harmondsworth: Penguin, 1968.

Gooding, C. 2000: Disability Discrimination Act: from statute to practice. *Critical Social Policy*, 20 (4), 533–49.

Goodley, D. 2000: *Self Advocacy in the Lives of People with Learning Difficulties: The Politics of Resilience.* Buckingham: Open University Press.

Gould, S. 1980: *The Panda's Thumb.* Harmondsworth: Penguin.

Gramsci, A. 1971: *Selections from the Prison Notebooks of Antonio Gramsci*, ed. and trans. Q. Hoare and G. Nowell-Smith. London: Lawrence and Wishart.

Gramsci, A. 1985: *Selections from the Cultural Writings*, ed. and trans. D. Forgacs and G. Nowell-Smith. London: Lawrence and Wishart.

Gregory, S. and Hartley, G. (eds) 1991: *Constructing Deafness.* London: Pinter/the Open University.

Groce, N. 1985: *Everyone Here Speaks Sign Language: Hereditary Deafness on Martha's Vineyard.* Cambridge, MA: Harvard University Press.

Gussow, Z. and Tracey, G. 1968: Status, ideology and adaptation to stigmatised illness. *Human Organisation*, 27, 316–25.

Haber, L. D. and Smith, R. T. 1971: Disability and deviance: normative adaptations of role behaviour. *American Sociological Review*, 36, 87–97.

Habermas, J. 1981: New social movements. *Telos*, 49, 33–7.

Hahn, H. 1986: Disability and the urban environment: a perspective on Los Angeles. *Environments and Planning D: Society and Space*, 4, 273–88.

Hahn, H. 1987: Civil rights for disabled Americans: the foundation of a political agenda. In A. Gartner and T. Joe (eds), *Images of the Disabled, Disabling Images*, New York: Praeger, 181–203.

Hahn, H. 1989: Disability and the reproduction of bodily images: the dynamics of human appearances. In J. Wolch and M. Dear (eds), *The Power of Geography*, Boston: Unwin Hyman, 370–89.

Hall, S. 1980: Encoding/decoding. In S. Hall et al. (eds), *Culture, Media, Language*, London: Hutchinson, 128–38.

Hall, S. 1988: New ethnicities. In K. Mercer (ed.), *Black Film, British Cinema*, London: Institute of Contemporary Arts, 27–31.

Hall, S. (ed.) 1997: *Representation: Cultural Representations and Signifying Practices.* London: Sage, in association with the Open University.

Hall, S. and Jefferson, T. (eds) 1976: *Resistance through Rituals.* London: Hutchinson.

Hanks, J. and Hanks, L. 1948: The physically handicapped in

certain non-Occidental societies. *Journal of Social Issues*, 4 (4), 11–20.

Haraway, D. 1990: *Simians, Cyborgs, and Women*. New York: Routledge.

Harris, J., Sapey, B. and Stewart, J. 1997: *Wheelchair Housing and the Estimation of Need*. Preston: University of Central Lancashire.

Harris, L. 1986: *The ICD Survey of Disabled Americans: Bringing Disabled Americans into the Mainstream*. New York: Louis Harris and Associates.

Held, D., McGrew, A., Goldblatt, D. and Perraton, J. 1999: *Global Transformation: Politics, Economics and Culture*. Cambridge: Polity.

Hevey, D. 1992: *The Creatures Time Forgot: Photography and Disability Imagery*. London: Routledge.

Higgins, P. C. 1981: *Outsiders in a Hearing World*. Beverly Hills, CA: Sage.

Hill, M. 1994: They are not our brothers: the Disability Movement and the Black Disability Movement. In N. Begum, M. Hill and A. Stevens (eds), *Reflections: Views of Black Disabled People on their Lives and Community Care*. London: Central Council for the Education and Training of Social Work, 68–80.

Hirsch, K. 1995: Culture and disability: the role of oral history. *Oral History Review*, 22 (1), 1–27.

Hirst, M. and Baldwin, S. 1995: *Unequal Opportunities: Growing Up Disabled*. York: Social Policy Research Unit, University of York.

Honey, S., Meager, N. and Williams, M. 1993: *Employers' Attitudes Towards People with Disabilities*. Brighton: Institute of Manpower Studies.

hooks, B. 1984: *Feminist Theory: From Margin to Centre*. Boston: South End Press.

Hughes, B. and Paterson, K. 1997: The social model of disability and the disappearing body: towards a sociology of impairment. *Disability and Society*, 12 (3), 325–40.

Humphrey, J. 1999: Disabled people and the politics of difference. *Disability and Society*, 14 (2), 173–88.

Humphries, S. and Gordon, P. 1992: *Out of Sight: The Experience of Disability 1900–1950*. London: Northcote House.

Hunt, P. 1966a: A critical condition. In P. Hunt (ed.), *Stigma: The Experience of Disability*, London: Geoffrey Chapman, 145–59.

Hunt, P. (ed.) 1966b: *Stigma: The Experience of Disability*. London: Geoffrey Chapman.

Hurst, R. 2000: To revise or not to revise. *Disability and Society*, 15 (7), 1083–7.

Hyde, M. 1996: Fifty years of failure: employment services for disabled people in the UK. *Work, Employment and Society*, 12, (4), 683–700.

Hyde, M. 1998: Sheltered and supported employment in the 1990s: the experience of disabled workers in the UK. *Disability and Society*, 13 (2), 199–216.

Illich, I. 1977a: Disabling professions. In I. Illich et al., *Disabling Professions*, London: Marion Boyars, 11–39.

Illich, I. 1977b: *Limits of Medicine, Medical Nemesis: The Expropriation of Health*. Harmondsworth: Penguin.

Illich, I., Zola, I. K., McKnight, J., Caplan, J. and Shaiken, H. 1977: *Disabling Professions*. London: Marion Boyars.

Imrie, R. F. 1996: *Disability and the City: International Perspectives*. London: Paul Chapman.

Imrie, R. F. and Wells, P. E. 1993: Disablism, planning and the built environment. *Environment and Planning C: Government and Policy*, 11 (2), 213–31.

Ingleby, D. (ed.) 1981: *Critical Psychiatry*. Harmondsworth: Penguin.

Ingleby, D. 1983: Mental health and social order. In S. Cohen and A. Scull (eds), *Social Control and the State*, Oxford: Blackwell, 141–88.

Inglis, F. 1993: *Cultural Studies*. Oxford: Blackwell.

Ingstad, B. 2001: Disability in the Developing World. In G. L. Albrecht, K. D. Seelman and M. Bury (eds), *Handbook of Disability Studies*, London: Sage, 772–92.

Ingstad, B. and Whyte, S. R. (eds) 1995: *Disability and Culture*. Berkeley: University of California Press.

Jayasooria, D. and Ooi, G. 1994: Disabled Peoples Movement in Malaysia. *Disability and Society*, 9 (1), 97–100.

Jenkins, R. 1991: Disability and social stratification. *British Journal of Sociology*, 42 (4), 557–80.

Jewson, N. 1976: The disappearance of the sick man from medical cosmology 1770–1870. *Sociology*, 10, 225–44.

Jones, M. and Marks, L. A. B. 1999: Law and the social construction of disability. In M. Jones and L. A. B. Marks (eds), *Disability, Divers-ability and Legal Change*, The Hague: Kluwer Law International/Martinus Nijhoff Publishers, 1–24.

Kalyanpur, M. 1996: The influences of Western special education on community-based services in India. *Disability and Society*, 11 (2), 249–69.

Karpf, A. 1988: *Doctoring the Media*. London: Routledge.

Kaye, H. S. 1997: *Education of Children with Disabilities*, abstract 19. San Francisco: Disability Statistics Center, University of California.

Kaye, H. S. 1998: *Is the Status of People with Disabilities Improving?*, abstract 21. San Francisco: Disability Statistics Center, University of California.

Kaye, H. S. 2000: *Computer and Internet Use among People with Disabilities*, Disability Statistics Report, No. 13. Washington, DC: US Department of Education, National Institute on Disability and Rehabilitation Research.

Kellner, D. 1989: *Critical Theory, Marxism and Modernity*. Cambridge: Polity.

Kelly, M. 1996: Negative attributes of self: radical surgery and the inner and outer life-world. In C. Barnes and G. Mercer (eds), *Exploring the Divide: Illness and Disability*, Leeds: Disability Press, 74–93.

Kent, D. 1987: Disabled women: portraits in fiction and drama. In A. Gartner and T. Joe (eds), *Images of the Disabled, Disabling Images*, London: Praeger, 47–63.

Kevles, D. J. 1985: *In the Name of Eugenics: Genetics and the Uses of Human Heredity*. New York: Alfred A. Knopf.

Kittay, E. F. 2001: When caring is just and justice is caring: justice and mental retardation. *Public Culture*, 13 (3), 557–79.

Kitzinger, J. 1993: Media messages and what people know about Acquired Immune Deficiency Syndrome. In Glasgow University Media Group, *Getting the Message*, London: Routledge, 271–304.

Klobas, L. E. 1988: *Disability Drama in Television and Film*. Jefferson, NC: McFarland.

Kriegel, L. 1987: The cripple in literature. In A. Gartner and T. Joe (eds), *Images of the Disabled, Disabling Images*, New York: Praeger, 31–46.

Kuper, A. 1999: *Culture: The Anthropologists' Account*. Cambridge, MA: Harvard University Press.

Ladd, P. 1988: Hearing impaired or British sign language users: social policies and the deaf community. *Disability, Handicap and Society*, 3 (2), 195–200.

Lamb, B. and Layzell, S. 1994: *Disabled in Britain: A World Apart*. London: SCOPE.

Lane, H. 1989: *When the Mind Hears: A History of the Deaf*. New York: Vintage Books.

Lane, H. 1995: Constructions of deafness. *Disability and Society*, 10 (2), 171–89.

LaPlante, M. P., Kennedy, J., Kaye, H. S. and Wenger, B. L. 1996: *Disability and Employment*, abstract 11, January. University of California: Disability Statistics Center. http://dsc.uesf.edu./abs/ab11txt.htm.

Larson, M. S. 1977: *The Rise of Professionalism: A Sociological Analysis*. Berkeley: University of California Press.

Layder, D. 1997: *Modern Social Theory*. London: UCL Press.

Lemert, E. 1951: *Social Pathology*. New York: McGraw-Hill.

Linton, S. 1998: *Claiming Disability: Knowledge and Identity*. New York: New York University Press.

Locker, D. 1983: *Disability and Disadvantage*. London: Tavistock.

Longmore, P. K. 1987: Screening stereotypes: images of disabled people in television and motion pictures. In A. Gartner and T. Joe (eds), *Images of the Disabled, Disabling Images*, New York: Praeger, 65–78.

Longmore, P. K. 1995: The second phase: from disability rights to disability culture. *Disability Rag and ReSource*, 16, 4–11.

Longmore, P. K. 1997: Conspicuous contribution and American cultural dilemmas: telethon rituals of cleansing and renewal. In D. T. Mitchell and S. L. Snyder (eds), *The Body and Physical Difference: Discourses of Disability*, Ann Arbor: University of Michigan Press, 134–58.

Longmore, P. K. and Goldberger, D. 2000: The League of the Physically Handicapped and the Great Depression: a case study in the new disability history. *Journal of American History*, 87 (3), 888–922.

Lonsdale, S. 1990: *Women and Disability: The Experience of Physical Disability among Women*. Basingstoke: Macmillan.

McQuail, D. (ed.) 1972: *Sociology of Mass Communications: Selected Readings*. Harmondsworth: Penguin.

Marconis, J. J. and Plummer, K. 1997: *Sociology: A Global Introduction*. London: Prentice-Hall Europe.

Marks, D. 2000: Secure base? Disabling design. In L. McKie and N. Watson (eds), *Organising Bodies: Policy, Institutions and Work*, Basingstoke: Macmillan, 42–53.

Marshall, T. H. 1950: *Citizenship and Social Class*. Cambridge: Cambridge University Press.

Martin, J. P. 1985: *Hospitals in Trouble*. Oxford: Blackwell.

Martin, J. P. and White, A. 1988: *OPCS Surveys of Disability in Great Britain, Report 2: The Financial Circumstances of Disabled Adults Living In Private Households*. London: HMSO.

Martin, J., White, A. and Meltzer, H. 1989: *OPCS Surveys of Disability in Great Britain, Report 4: Disabled Adults: Services, Transport and Employment*. London: HMSO.

Mason, M. 1990: Internalised oppression. In R. Rieser and M. Mason (eds), *Disability Quality in the Classroom: A Human Rights Issue*, London: Inner London Education Authority, 27–8.

Maynard, M. 1994: Methods, practice and epistemology: the debate about feminism and research. In M. Maynard and J. Purvis (eds), *Researching Women's Lives from a Feminist Perspective*, London: Taylor and Francis, 10–26.

Meager, N. et al. 1999: *Monitoring the Disability Discrimination Act (DDA) 1995.* London: Department of Education and Employment.

Meekosha, H. and Dowse, L. 1997: Distorting images, invisible images: gender, disability and the media. *Media International Australia,* 84 (May), 91–101.

Melucci, A. 1989: *Nomads of the Present: Social Movements and Individual Needs in Contemporary Society.* London: Hutchinson.

Miles, M. 1992: Concepts of mental retardation in Pakistan: toward cross-cultural and historical perspectives. *Disability, Handicap and Society,* 7 (3), 235–55.

Miles, M. 1995: Disability in an eastern religious context: historical perspectives. *Disability and Society,* 10 (1), 49–69.

Miles, S. 1996: Engaging with the disability rights movement: the experience of community-based rehabilitation in Southern Africa. *Disability and Society,* 11 (4), 501–17.

Miller, E. J. and Gwynne, G. V. 1972: *A Life Apart.* London: Tavistock.

Miller, P. and Rose, N. (eds) 1988: *The Power of Psychiatry,* Cambridge: Polity.

Mills, C. Wright 1963: *Power, Politics and People: The Collected Essays of C. Wright Mills.* New York: Ballantine Books.

Mills, C. Wright 1970: *The Sociological Imagination.* Harmondsworth: Penguin.

Minde, K. S. 1972: How they grow up: forty-one physically handicapped children and their families. *American Journal of Psychiatry,* 128, 1554–60.

Mitchell, D. T. and Snyder, S. L. 2001: Representation and its discontents. In G. L. Albrecht, K. D. Seelman and M. Bury (eds), *Handbook of Disability Studies,* London: Sage, 195–218.

Morris, J. 1989: *Able Lives – Women's Experience of Paralysis.* London: Women's Press.

Morris, J. 1991: *Pride Against Prejudice: Transforming Attitudes to Disability.* London: Women's Press.

Morris, J. 1993a: Feminism and disability. *Feminist Review,* 43, 57–70.

Morris, J. 1993b: *Independent Lives? Community Care and Disabled People.* Basingstoke: Macmillan.

Morris, J. 1997: Gone missing? Disabled children living away from their families. *Disability and Society,* 12 (2), 241–58.

Morrison, K. and Finkelstein, V. 1993: Broken arts and cultural repair: the role of culture in the empowerment of disabled people. In J. Swain, V. Finkelstein, S. French and M. Oliver (eds), *Disabling Barriers – Enabling Environments,* London: Sage in association with the Open University, 122–27.

Mulvany, J. 2000: Disability, impairment or illness? The relevance of the social model of disability to the study of mental disorder. *Sociology of Health and Illness*, 22 (5), 582–601.

Murphy, R. 1987: *The Body Silent*. London: Phoenix House.

National Council on Disability 2000a: *From Privileges to Rights: People Labeled with Psychiatric Disabilities Speak for Themselves*. Washington, DC: National Council on Disability. http://www.ncd.gov.

National Council on Disability 2000b: *Promises to Keep: A Decade of Federal Enforcement of the Americans with Disabilities Act*. Washington, DC: National Council on Disability. http://www.ncd.gov.

New Internationalist 1992: Disabled lives: difference and defiance. No. 233, July (special issue).

Nicolaisen, I. 1995: Persons and nonpersons: disability and personhood among the Punan Bah of Central Borneo. In B. Ingstad and S. R. Whyte (eds), *Disability and Culture*, Berkeley: University of California Press, 38–55.

NIDRR 2000: *Long Range Plan*. Washington, DC: US Department of Education, National Institute on Disability and Rehabilitation Research.

Norden, M. 1994: *The Cinema of Isolation: A History of Disability in the Movies*. New Brunswick, NJ: Rutgers University Press.

Oliver, M. 1983: *Social Work with Disabled People*. Basingstoke: Macmillan.

Oliver, M. 1990: *The Politics of Disablement*. Basingstoke: Macmillan.

Oliver, M. 1996a: Defining impairment and disability: issues at stake. In C. Barnes and G. Mercer (eds), *Exploring the Divide: Illness and Disability*, Leeds: Disability Press, 39–54.

Oliver, M. 1996b: A sociology of disability or a disablist sociology? In L. Barton (ed.), *Disability and Society: Emerging Issues and Insights*, London: Longman, 18–42.

Oliver, M. 1996c: *Understanding Disability: From Theory to Practise*. Basingstoke: Macmillan.

Oliver, M. and Barnes, C. 1998: *Social Policy and Disabled People: From Exclusion to Inclusion*. London: Longman.

Oliver, M., Zarb, G., Silver, J., Moore, M. and Salisbury, V. 1988: *Walking into Darkness: The Experience of Spinal Injury*. Basingstoke: Macmillan.

Padden, C. and Humphries, T. 1988: *Deaf in America: Voices from a Culture*. Cambridge, MA: Harvard University Press.

Pagel, M. 1988: *On Our Own Behalf: An Introduction to the Self Organisation of Disabled People*. Manchester: Greater Manchester Coalition of Disabled People Publications.

Parker, R. A. 1988: An historical background. In National Institute for Social Work/I. Sinclair (ed.), *Residential Care: The Research Reviewed*, London: HMSO, 1–38.

Parsons, T. 1951: *The Social System*. New York: Free Press.

Paterson, K. and Hughes, G. 1999a: Disability studies and phenomenology: the carnal politics of everyday life. *Disability and Society*, 14 (5), 597–610.

Paterson, K. and Hughes, G. 1999b: Disabled bodies. In P. Hancock et al. (eds), *The Body, Culture and Society: An Introduction*, Buckingham: Open University Press, 29–44.

Pelling, M. 1998: *The Common Lot: Sickness, Medical Occupations and the Urban Poor in Early Modern England*. London: Longman.

Peters, S. 2000: Is there a disability culture? A syncretisation of three possible world views. *Disability and Society*, 15 (4), 583–601.

Pfeiffer, D. 1994: The Americans with Disabilities Act: costly mandates or civil rights. *Disability and Society*, 9 (4), 533–42.

Philo, G. (ed.) 1996: *Media and Mental Distress*. Harlow: Addison Wesley Longman.

Pointon, A. 1997: Rights of access. In A. Pointon and C. Davies (eds), *Framed: Interrogating Disability in the Media*, London: British Film Institute, 234–40.

Pointon, A. 1999: Out of the closet: new images of disability in the civil rights campaign. In B. Franklin (ed.), *Social Policy, the Media and Misrepresentation*, London: Routledge, 222–37.

Pointon, A. and Davies, C. (eds) 1997: *Framed: Interrogating Disability in the Media*. London: British Film Institute.

Price, J. and Shildrick, M. 1998: Uncertain thoughts on the disabled body. In M. Shildrick and J. Price (eds), *Vital Signs: Feminist Reconfigurations of the Biological Body*, Edinburgh: Edinburgh University Press, 224–49.

Priestley, M. 1999: *Disability Politics and Community Care*. London: Jessica Kingsley.

Priestley, M. 2000: Adults only: disability, social policy and the life course. *Journal of Social Policy*, 29 (3), 421–39.

Priestley, M. (ed.) 2001: *Disability and the Life Course: Global Perspectives*. Cambridge: Cambridge University Press.

Quicke, J. C. (1985): *Disability in Modern Children's Fiction*. London: Croom Helm.

Radford, J. P. 1994: Intellectual disability and the heritage of modernity. In M. H. Rioux and M. Bach (eds), *Disability Is Not Measles: New Research Paradigms in Disability*, North York, Ontario: Roeher Institute, 9–27.

Radley, A. and Green, R. 1987: Illness as adjustment: a methodology and conceptual framework. *Sociology of Health and Illness*, 9, 197–207.

Rioux, M. H., Crawford, C., Ticoll, M. and Bach, M. 1997: Uncovering the shape of violence: a research methodology rooted in the experience of people with disabilities. In C. Barnes and G. Mercer (eds), *Doing Disability Research*, Leeds: Disability Press, 190–206.

Robson, P., Locke, M. and Dawson, J. 1977: *Consumerism or Democracy: User Involvement in the Control of Voluntary Organisations*. Bristol: Policy Press.

Rock, P. 1996: Eugenics and euthanasia: a cause for concern for disabled people, particularly disabled women. *Disability and Society*, 11 (1), 121–7.

Rose, N. 1990: *Governing the Soul*. London: Routledge.

Ross, K. 1997: *Disability and Broadcasting: A View from the Margins*. Cheltenham: Cheltenham and Gloucester College of Higher Education.

Roulstone, A. 1998: *Enabling Technology: Disabled People, Work and New Technology*. Buckingham: Open University Press.

Rowe, A. (ed.) 1990: *Lifetime Homes: Flexible Housing for Successive Generations*. London: Helen Hamlyn Foundation.

Russell, M. 1998: *Beyond Ramps: Disability at the End of the Social Contract*. Monroe: Common Courage Press.

Ryan, J. with Thomas, F. 1980: *The Politics of Mental Handicap*. Harmondsworth: Penguin.

Safilios-Rothschild, C. 1970: *The Sociology and Social Psychology of Disability and Rehabilitation*. New York: Random House.

Sapey, B. 2000: Disablement in the Informational Age. *Disability and Society*, 15 (4), 619–36.

Saxton, M. and Howe, F. (eds) 1988: *With Wings: An Anthology of Literature by Women with Disabilities*. London: Virago.

Sayce, L. 2000: *From Psychiatric Patient to Citizen: Overcoming Discrimination and Exclusion*. Basingstoke: Macmillan.

Scambler, G. and Hopkins, A. 1986: Being epileptic: coming to terms with stigma. *Sociology of Health and Illness*, 8, 26–43.

Scheer, J. and Groce, N. 1988: Impairment as a human constant: cross-cultural and historical perspectives on variation. *Journal of Social Issues*, 44 (1), 23–37.

Scheff, T. J. 1966: *Being Mentally Ill*. New York: Aldine.

Scheper-Hughes, N. 1992: *Death without Weeping: The Violence of Everyday Life in Brazil*. Berkeley: University of California Press.

Schneider, J. W. and Conrad, P. 1983: *Having Epilepsy: The Experience and Control of Epilepsy*. Philadelphia: Temple University Press.

Scotch, R. 1988: Disability as the basis for a social movement: advocacy and the politics of definition. *Journal of Social Issues*, 44 (1), 159–72.

Scott, A. 1990: *Ideology and New Social Movements*. London: Unwin Hyman.

Scott, R. A. 1969: *The Making of Blind Men*. London: Sage.

Scott, R. and Morris, G. 2001: *Polls Apart 3: Campaigning for Accessible Democracy*. London: Scope.

Scull, A. 1979: *Museums of Madness*. London: Allen Lane.

Scull, A. 1984: *Decarceration: Community Treatment and the Deviant – A Radical View*, 2nd edn. Cambridge: Polity.

Seymour, W. 1998: *Remaking the Body: Rehabilitation and Change*. London: Routledge.

Shakespeare, T. 1992: A response to Liz Crow. *Coalition*, September, 40–2.

Shakespeare, T. 1993: Disabled people's self-organisation: a new social movement? *Disability, Handicap and Society*, 8 (3), 249–63.

Shakespeare, T. 1994: Cultural representation of disabled people: dustbins for disavowal? *Disability and Society*, 9 (3), 283–99.

Shakespeare, T. 1999: Art and lies? Representations of disability on film. In M. Corker and S. French (eds), *Disability Discourse*, Buckingham: Open University Press, 164–72.

Shakespeare, T., Gillespie-Sells, K. and Davies, D. 1996: *The Sexual Politics of Disability: Untold Desires*. London: Cassell.

Shapiro, J. P. 1993: *No Pity: People with Disabilities Forging a New Civil Rights Movement*. New York: Times Books.

Shearer, A. 1981: *Disability: Whose Handicap?* Oxford: Blackwell.

Shildrick, M. and Price, J. 1996: Breaking the boundaries of the broken body. *Body and Society*, 2 (4), 93–113.

Shilling, C. 1993: *The Body and Social Theory*. London: Sage.

Skeggs, B. 1995: Introduction. In B. Skeggs (ed.), *Feminist Cultural Theory: Process and Production*, Manchester: Manchester University Press, 1–29.

Smith, S. and Jordan, A. 1991: *What the Papers Say and Don't Say about Disability*. London: Spastics Society.

Snyder, S. L. and Mitchell, D. T. 2001: Re-engaging the body: disability studies and the resistance to embodiment. *Public Culture*, 13 (3), 367–89.

Sobsey, R. 1994: *Violence and Abuse in the Lives of People with Disabilities*. London and Baltimore: Brookes Publishing.

Soder, M. 1989: Disability as a social construct: the labelling approach revisited. *European Journal of Special Needs Education*, 4 (2), 117–29.

Somers, M. 1994: The narrative construction of identity: a relational and network approach. *Theory and Society*, 23, 605–49.

Sontag, S. 1991: *Illness as Metaphor: Aids and its Metaphors.* Hanmondsworth: Penguin.

Stacey, J. 1997: Feminist theory: capital F, capital T. In V. Robinson and D. Richardson (eds), *Introducing Women's Studies*, 2nd edn, Basingstoke: Macmillan, 54–76.

Stalker, K., Barron, S., Riddell, S. and Wilkinson, H. 1999: Models of disability: the relationship between theory and practice in non-statutory organisations. *Critical Social Policy*, 19 (1), 5–29.

Stanley, N., Manthorpe, J. and Penhale, B. (eds) 1999: *Institutional Abuse: Perspectives across the Life Course.* London: Routledge.

Steinberg, D. L. 1997: *Bodies in Glass: Genetics, Eugenics and Embryo Ethics.* Manchester: Manchester University Press.

Stiker, H.-J. 1999: *A History of Disability*, trans. W. Sayers. Ann Arbor: University of Michigan Press.

Stone, D. A. 1985: *The Disabled State.* Basingstoke: Macmillan.

Stone, E. 1999a: Disability and development in the majority world. In E. Stone (ed.), *Disability and Development*, Leeds: Disability Press, 1–18.

Stone, E. 1999b: Modern slogan, ancient script: impairment and disability in the Chinese language. In M. Corker and S. French (eds), *Disability Discourse*, Buckingham: Open University Press, 136–47.

Strong, P. 1979: Sociological imperialism and the profession of medicine: a critical examination of the thesis of medical imperialism. *Social Science and Medicine*, 13A (2), 199–215.

Stuart, O. 1993: Double oppression: an appropriate starting-point? In J. Swain, V. Finkelstein, S. French and M. Oliver (eds), *Disabling Barriers – Enabling Environments*, London: Sage, 93–100.

Sutherland, D. 1997: Disability arts and disability politics. In A. Pointon and C. Davies (eds), *Framed: Interrogating Disability in the Media*, London: British Film Institute, 159.

Swain, J. and French, S. 2000: Towards an affirmative model of disability. *Disability and Society*, 15 (4), 569–82.

Szasz, T. S. 1971: *The Manufacture of Madness.* London: Routledge and Kegan Paul.

Talle, A. 1995: A child is a child: disability and equality among the Kenya Masai. In B. Ingstad and S. R. Whyte (eds), *Disability and Culture*, Berkeley: University of California Press, 56–72.

Thomas, A. P., Bax, M. C. O. and Smythe, D. P. L. 1989: *The Health and Social Needs of Young Adults with Physical Disabilities.* Oxford: Blackwell Scientific Publications.

Thomas, C. 1997: The baby and the bathwater: disabled women and motherhood in social context. *Sociology of Health and Illness*, 19 (5), 622–43.

Thomas, C. 1999: *Female Forms: Experiencing and Understanding Disability*. Buckingham: Open University Press.

Thomas, D. 1982: *The Experience of Handicap*. London: Methuen.

Thomas, M. and Thomas, M. J. 2002: A discussion of some controversies in community based rehabilitation. *Asia Pacific Disability Rehabilitation Journal*, 13 (1), 2–10.

Thomson, R. G. (ed.) 1996: *Freakery: Cultural Spectacles of the Extraordinary Body*. New York: Columbia University Press.

Thomson, R. G. 1997: *Extraordinary Bodies: Figuring Physical Disability in American Culture and Literature*. New York: Columbia University Press.

Thornton, P., Sainsbury, R. and Barnes, H. 1997: *Helping Disabled People to Work: A Cross National Study of Social Security and Employment Provision*. London: The Stationary Office.

Tomlinson, A. (ed.) 1990: *Consumption, Identity and Style*. London: Routledge.

Tomlinson, S. 1982: *A Sociology of Special Education*. London: Routledge and Kegan Paul.

Tomlinson, S. 1996: Conflicts and dilemmas for professionals in special education. In C. Christensen and F. Rizvi (eds), *Disability and the Dilemmas of Education and Justice*, Buckingham: Open University Press, 175–86.

Topliss, E. 1982: *Social Responses to Handicap*. London: Longman.

Touraine, A. 1981: *The Voice and the Eye: An Analysis of Social Movements*. Cambridge: Cambridge University Press.

Townsend, P. 1967: *The Last Refuge*. London: Routlege and Kegan Paul.

Tremain, S. 1996: *Pushing the Limits: Disabled Dykes Produce Culture*. Toronto: Women's Press.

Tremblay, M. 1996: Going back to civvy street: a historical account of the Everest and Jennings wheelchair for Canadian World War II veterans with spinal chord injury. *Disability and Society*, 11 (2), 149–69.

Trent, J. W. 1994: *Inventing the Feeble Mind: A History of Mental Retardation in the United States*. Berkeley: University of California Press.

Turner, B. S. 1984: *The Body and Society*. Oxford: Blackwell.

Turner, B. S. 1987: *Medical Power and Social Knowledge*. London: Sage.

Turner, B. S. 1992: *Regulating Bodies: Essays in Medical Sociology*. London: Routledge.

UNESCO 1994: *The Salamanca Statement and Framework for Action on Special Needs Education: World Conference on Special Needs Education*. New York: UNESCO.

UNESCO 1995: *Overcoming Obstacles to the Integration of Disabled People*. London: Disability Awareness in Action.

United Nations 1971: *Declaration on the Rights of Mentally Retarded Persons*. New York: United Nations.

United Nations 1975: *Declaration of the Rights of Disabled Persons*. New York: United Nations.

United Nations 1990: *Disability Statistics Compendium*. New York: United Nations Statistics Office.

United Nations 1993: *Standard Rules on the Equalization of Opportunities for Persons with Disabilities*. New York: United Nations.

UPIAS 1976: *Fundamental Principles of Disability*. London: Union of the Physically Impaired Against Segregation.

Vasey, S. 1992: A Response to Liz Crow. *Coalition*, September, 42–4.

Vernon, A. 1999: The dialectics of multiple identities and the disabled people's movement. *Disability and Society*, 14 (3), 385–98.

Walker, Alan 1982: *Unqualified and Underemployed: Handicapped Young People in the Labour Market*. Basingstoke: Macmillan.

Walker, A. and Walker, C. 1998: Normalisation and 'normal' ageing: the social construction of dependency among older people with learning difficulties. *Disability and Society*, 13 (1), 125–42.

Walker, Andrew 1995: Universal access and the built environment – or from glacier to garden gate. In G. Zarb (ed.), *Removing Disabling Barriers*, London: Policy Studies Institute, 38–48.

Walmsley, J. 1997: Including people with learning difficulties: theory and practice. In L. Barton and M. Oliver (eds), *Disability Studies: Past, Present and Future*, Leeds: Disability Press, 62–77.

Warnock 1978: *Report of the Committee of Enquiry into the Education of Handicapped Children and Young People*. London: HMSO.

Weller, D. J. and Miller, P. M. 1977: Emotional reactions of patients, family and staff in acute care period of spinal cord injury: part 1. *Social Work in Health Care*, 2 (4), 369–77.

Wells, H. G. 1979: *The Complete Short Stories of H. G. Wells*. London: Ernest Benn Limited.

Wendell, S. 1989: Towards a feminist theory of disability. *Hypatia*, 4 (Summer), 10–24.

Wendell, S. 1996: *The Rejected Body: Feminist Philosophical Reflections on Disability*. London: Routledge.

Westcott, H. and Cross, M. 1996: *This Far and No Further: Towards the Ending of the Abuse of Disabled Children*. Birmingham: Venture Press.

WHO 1980: *International Classification of Impairments, Disabilities and Handicaps*. Geneva: World Health Organization.

WHO 1999: *International Classification of Functioning and Disability, Beta-2 draft, Short Version.* Geneva: World Health Organization.

WHO 2001: *Rethinking Care from Disabled People's Perspectives.* Geneva: World Health Organization.

Williams, F. 1992: Somewhere over the rainbow: universality and diversity in social policy. In N. Manning and R. Page (eds), *Social Policy Review*, No. 4, Canterbury, Social Policy Association, 200–19.

Williams, G. 1984a: The genesis of chronic illness: narrative reconstruction. *Sociology of Health and Illness*, 6 (2), 175–200.

Williams, G. 1984b: The Movement for Independent Living: an evaluation and critique. *Social Science and Medicine*, 17 (15), 1000–12.

Williams, G. 1991: Disablement and the ideological crisis in health care. *Social Science and Medicine*, 32 (4), 517–24.

Williams, G. 1996: Representing disability: some questions of phenomenology and politics. In C. Barnes and G. Mercer (eds), *Exploring the Divide: Illness and Disability*, Leeds: Disability Press, 194–212.

Williams, G. 1998: The sociology of disability: towards a materialist phenomenology. In T. Shakespeare (ed.), *Disability Studies Reader*, London: Cassell, 234–44.

Williams, S. 2000: Chronic illness as biographical disruption or biographical disruption as chronic illness: perspectives on a core concept. *Sociology of Health and Illness*, 22 (1), 40–67.

Williams, S. and Bendelow, G. 1998: *The Lived Body: Sociological Themes, Embodied Issues.* London: Routledge.

Wilson, A. N. 1997: How not to win friends. *Sunday Telegraph*, 28 December.

Winzer, M. A. 1993: *The History of Special Education: From Isolation to Integration.* Washington, DC: Gallaudet University Press.

Wolch, J. and Dear, M. (eds) 1989: *The Power of Geography: How Territory Shapes Social Life.* Boston: Unwin Hyman.

Wolfensberger, W. 1989: Human service policies: The rhetoric versus the reality. In L. Barton (ed.), *Disability and Dependence*, Lewes: Falmer, 23–42.

Wolfensberger, W. and Thomas, S. 1983: *Program Analysis of Service Systems Implementation of Normalisation Goals: Normalisation and Ratings Manual*, 2nd edn. Toronto: National Institute of Mental Retardation.

Woodward, K. (ed.) 1997: *Identity and Difference.* London: Sage and Open University Press.

Young, I. M. 1990: *Justice and the Politics of Difference.* Princeton: Princeton University Press.

Young, I. M. 1997: Unruly categories: a critique of Nancy Fraser's dual systems theory. *New Left Review*, 222 (March/April), 147–60.

Zarb, G. and Oliver, M. 1992: *Ageing with a Disability: The Dimensions of Need*. London: Thames Polytechnic.

Zola, I. K. 1982: *Missing Pieces: A Chronicle of Living with a Disability*. Philadelphia: Temple University Press.

Zola, I. K. 1983: Developing new self-images and interdependence. In N. Crewe and I. K. Zola (eds), *Independent Living for Physically Disabled People*, London: Jossey Bass, 49–59.

Zola, I. K. 1985: Depictions of disability – metaphor, message, and medium in the media: a research and political agenda. *Social Science Journal*, 22 (4), 5–17.

Zola, I. K. 1993: Self identity and the naming question: reflections on the language of disability. *Social Science and Medicine*, 36, 167–73.

Zola, I. K. 1994: Towards inclusion: the role of people with disabilities in policy and research issues in the United States – a historical and political analysis. In M. H. Rioux and M. Bach (eds), *Disability Is Not Measles: New Research Paradigms in Disability*, North York, Ontario: Roeher Institute, 49–66.

Index